SINISTER CHICAGO

SINISTER CHICAGO
Windy City Secrets, Urban Legends, and Sordid Characters

KALI JOY CRAMER

Guilford, Connecticut

Globe Pequot

An imprint of The Rowman & Littlefield Publishing Group, Inc.
4501 Forbes Blvd., Ste. 200
Lanham, MD 20706
www.rowman.com

Distributed by NATIONAL BOOK NETWORK

British Library Cataloguing in Publication Information available

Library of Congress Cataloging-in-Publication Data
Names: Cramer, Kali Joy, 1994- author.
Title: Sinister Chicago : windy city secrets, urban legends, and sordid characters / Kali Joy Cramer.
Description: Guilford, Connecticut : Globe Pequot, [2020] | Includes bibliographical references. | Summary: "In Sinister Chicago, author Kali Cramer examines the legends behind some of Sin City's notorious characters—including H.H. Holmes, Al Capone, and John Wayne Gacy—as well as infamous landmarks and devastating tragedies, like the Great Chicago Fire and the Eastland shipwreck. Equal parts true crime and tragedy, Sinister Chicago chronicles the unknown, unusual, or otherwise unexplained events that helped shape the Windy City"— Provided by publisher.
Identifiers: LCCN 2020011132 (print) | LCCN 2020011133 (ebook) | ISBN 9781493045167 (trade paperback) | ISBN 9781493059607 (epub)
Subjects: LCSH: Crime—Illinois—Chicago—History. | Criminals—Illinois—Chicago—History.
Classification: LCC HV6795.C4 C73 2020 (print) | LCC HV6795.C4 (ebook) | DDC 364.109773/11—dc23
LC record available at https://lccn.loc.gov/2020011132
LC ebook record available at https://lccn.loc.gov/2020011133

Contents

Acknowledgments

Without the help of the Chicago Public Library, the *Chicago Tribune* Archives, the Chicago History Museum, and the Newberry Library, I would have had quite a rough time compiling all relevant information for this book. I am endlessly grateful to live in a city where knowledge is power and accessible to the public to such a great extent.

In addition to hard research, listening to some of my favorite podcasts on the way to work every morning was extremely helpful in uncovering the spellbinding details that made this book come alive. *My Favorite Murder*, *Female Criminals*, *Stuff You Missed in History Class*, and *Stuff You Should Know* were all vital resources in discovering stories I had never heard before. Thank you to the hosts, Karen Kilgariff and Georgia Hardstark, Vanessa Richardson and Sami Nye, Tracy V. Wilson and Holly Frey, and Josh Clark and Chuck Bryant, respectively, for your unusual fascination with the darker side of history.

Thank you also to my editor, Sarah Parke, at Globe Pequot Press, who took over for my original editor, Katherine O'Dell, halfway through. You both helped me cultivate the structure of these stories and gave me the guidance I needed to write my first book.

And, of course, my eternal gratitude goes out to my mom, a strongly vivacious heroine with powerful ambition and a deep wellspring of kindness and love. You were there when I wrote on the walls in first grade, when I received my first-ever bad grade on a college paper, and now, for my first publication. Thank you for sharpening me into a woman of your resilient and steadfast likeness.

Introduction

Everyone knows that the best view of the city is driving into it from Lake Shore Drive. North or south, no matter which neighborhood along the coast you're coming from, the city is most beautiful along the lakefront. The winding shore brings the faded buildings in and out of view until suddenly, they loom above you, the skyscrapers of the Windy City, the mountains of Illinois.

When I think of Chicago, I envision the gleaming lights off Navy Pier. I think about how every summer, North Avenue Beach turns into the largest party Chicago has ever seen. I think of Wrigley Field and how the Chicago Cubs finally laid the curse to rest when they became 2016 World Series champions. I think about the notable figures who made their start here: Kanye West and Jennifer Hudson and President Obama and the First Lady, Michelle. I think deep-dish pizza and Italian beef (extra wet) and a Chicago dog with absolutely no ketchup. I also think about how kind the people on the street can be every day.

Before last year, my heart was spellbound by Chicago's overwhelming magnificence, naive to its disturbing past and fiercely loyal to the namesake of the city. Now I recognize that every hometown has its horrors. Chicago looms over the Midwest like an iron giant, ready to take on anyone or anything that stands in the way of its might and everlasting glory. Many see this place as a sanctuary, a safe haven, a home, while others recognize that there are dark secrets lurking in every corner of Chicago's murky, if shallow, history. Researching these underground stories compelled me to fall in love with this city all over again. Every story brought me to a new place as I walked the paths that Chicago's greatest villains had tramped before me, exploring my tainted city with an ominous historical perspective for the first time.

The real-life Gotham City has corrupt origins just like its fictional counterpart, ones that people have only guessed at or not bothered to look straight in the face for fear of the truth. And, while all of this strangeness certainly makes Chicago the intriguing cesspool of secrets that it is today, it's easy to feel disturbed in the wake of the monumental tragedies, horrors, and otherwise unexplained events that plague this city's history.

Everyone is interested in the shocking, whether they care to admit it or not. I am no exception to having a casual curiosity about morbid stories. After diving into some of the strangest secrets that Chicago had for an editorial, an interest in the weird gripped me. Globe Pequot Press gave me the platform to expand on these unusual tales, which manifested into traversing the darker side of Chicago history, starting, of course, with Chicago's most infamous characters.

Throughout the first part of the book, you'll find yourself chilled by serial killers like H. H. Holmes and John Wayne Gacy, staring down the barrel of Al Capone's gun, and cavorting in the Levee District with the Everleigh sisters.

Chicago was filled to the brim with ominous outlaws who pushed the boundaries of society, some with more malicious intentions than others. As you watch Dillinger weave in and out of the city and question the morality of the Lipstick Killer, notice how every one of these criminals carries notoriety, but not all have wicked objectives.

The second part of *Sinister Chicago* tackles the difficult process of selecting the most horrendous tragedies Chicago has ever seen. While both the first and third parts of the book include stories of murder, violence, and rape, the singular events described in the second part stand out as the most tragic and unjust. The conclusions of these stories fluctuate wildly, from moments where humanity rose from the ashes to events that fostered death and despair. Chicago's sinister history extends into both historical erasure and accidents that should never have happened.

There are plenty of landmarks still standing in Chicago that are soaked in rich history, a few of which have particularly corrupt narratives. Elements of creepy take over some stories, from the morbid fire in the Loop to what lurks beneath Lincoln Park, and systematic immorality plagues others, like the extensive history of Chicago's first slum. Chances are you've been here before, and your perspective will change after you discover the sinister history behind it.

What a shame to know the truth, that the White City is soaked crimson with bloodshed and injustice. Chicago might not exist the same today if these macabre events had not occurred, but I deeply mourn the victims of the past. So many innocent people were caught in the crossfire of

American history and I have no words that could possibly right the wrongs built into their stories.

But there is hope. Chicago is now a glistening city, made up of a vastly diverse group of people who enhance its cultural richness. There will always remain an effort to ward off evil, construct more sensible laws, and protect the people of this city, but we are fighting for the safety and happiness that all of us deserve. Chicago is brimming with warriors who are working endlessly to reduce criminal activity, including ordinary people who practice kindness in everyday life. With these efforts, we can only hope the world is a better place tomorrow than it is today.

As the bitter wind picks up and carries you along Lake Shore Drive into some of the most historic landmarks that Chicago has to offer, keep in mind the glistening future of this great city. Let not these dark histories take hold of your soul and send you into despair. Tomorrow is bright. Chicago still stands. And its secrets do not define its future.

Part I
Chicago's Infamous Characters

Wanted poster for John Dillinger, displaying his fingerprints, signature, and portrait, 1934. EVERETT HISTORICAL/SHUTTERSTOCK.COM

CHAPTER ONE

H. H. Holmes

Born with the Devil Inside

CHICAGO WAS AT THE HEIGHT OF INNOVATION WHEN THE devil arrived.

He was an irresistible figure, towering above the average man and effortlessly smooth. While men only dreamt of growing the full, bristling mustache that concealed his lips, women found him inexplicably alluring. But in the end, they all fell victim to his horror.

The devil entered Chicago as the city was reaching its prime by hosting the world's fair, then known as the Columbian Exposition. It was the most anticipated event of the year, and it offered a way for inventors to introduce many new things to the world. People traveled from every corner of the earth to see inventions that are commonplace today—like the first gas-powered motor, the zipper, and Pabst Blue Ribbon beer. When Chicago outbid New York to host the Columbian Exposition, *New York Sun* editor Charles Dana implored his readers to ignore the "nonsensical claims of that windy city," unintentionally inventing the famous nickname. Of course, the world's fair was also where George Washington Gale Ferris Jr. revealed his enormous, spinning wheel, one of which can be found in almost every amusement park in the world today. There was even a 1,500-pound chocolate statue of the Venus de Milo looming over the courtyard as people gazed up in awe.

But among the many amazing and never-before-seen attractions that awaited the guests who had traveled from Chicago and beyond to explore the fair, there lurked a serial murderer whose sinister invention would become known as H. H. Holmes's Murder Castle.

Though the building seemed to serve as a line of retail stores topped by residential apartments, which were used as surplus hotel rooms for world's fair guests, a series of unusually malicious features were built into the plans at 63rd Street and Wallace Avenue. The first and second floors, for instance, were connected by a private compartment and staircase that Holmes used to travel in secret. Most of Holmes's employees knew of the passageway and thought nothing of it. What they didn't know was that Holmes used this method of creeping, along with many other hidden avenues in the building, to prey on the innocent, quenching some sick satisfaction in removing them from his path. Deadly secrets crawled the walls of Murder Castle, all sadistically perpetuated by the devil himself, and almost no one coaxed inside ever returned.

Many of the rooms were soundproof, but guests didn't know that when they checked into the upstairs hotel. Instead, the horror set in when they awoke to the smell of gas leaking through wall vents in the middle of the night. But by then, it was too late to escape. Holmes was ready to start his work. No longer guests, but prisoners, they would often find their doors locked, but even if they could get out, they were met with secret passageways that led nowhere. The building was riddled with windowless rooms and trapdoors that led to airtight chambers with iron-plated walls. Many of the features were controllable by levers and pulleys in Holmes's office, and he even installed a bell that was triggered when guests would step outside of their rooms.

Holmes played with his victims, often waiting until they were shrieking for help before he gave lenience. His version of grace, however, was to get the victims where he wanted them and then drop the floor out from under them. There was one section of the second floor that had a wooden chute leading straight to the basement, a nightmarish ending for Holmes's most unfortunate victims. Many fell to their deaths down the chute, but the unluckiest were finished off in acid vats and pits of quicklime.

There was a crematorium in the basement used to dispose of the remaining evidence and an operating table stood close, always blood-soaked and awaiting the next to suffer. Nearby lay an ominous spread of surgical tools and a strange torture device, all used to dissect and strip the cadavers down to bone. Holmes would sell the skeletons to universities, making a profit off of his sins.

And yet, during all his time in Chicago, no one ever accused H. H. Holmes of murder or harmful intent. Several people went missing after coming in contact with Holmes, and even if the victims' loved ones made this connection in their heads, they never came forward or made an effort to stop the violence. Holmes played them all so well that his charm, however staged, made a lasting impression. The devil almost walked free.

Before Chicago ever called to H. H. Holmes, he was born Herman Webster Mudgett to affluent Methodist parents in Gilmanton, New Hampshire, on May 16, 1861. Journalists have since mythicized his household situation, claiming that his father was recklessly brutal in the home and that Holmes may have tortured and experimented on small animals as a child. Such stories are the product of modern media attempting to fit Holmes into the mold of the contemporary serial killer, but the truth is he doesn't fit. Herman Webster Mudgett was given love, care, attention, and a grand education, but he still had the greedy nerve to demand more of the world. Holmes wouldn't stay in New Hampshire for long, and when he left, he would evolve into America's most infamous terror, deserving of the White City Devil moniker.

One of the few boys Holmes befriended in his childhood was an older kid named Tom. When Holmes was eleven, the two boys went exploring inside an abandoned home riddled with rotting floorboards and dilapidated walls. Tom fell to his death from a landing on the second floor; at the time, both families believed his death was a tragic accident. In hindsight, it is far more likely that Tom was Holmes's very first victim.

Holmes married three times in his life, but not all of these unions were legally recognized, as Holmes didn't bother to get divorced when he skipped town. All his wives assumed they were still technically wed after Holmes left them. And he did always leave them. He first stole the heart of Clara Lovering when they were barely seventeen, even fathering a child with her. The family moved out of state so that Holmes could study medicine at the University of Vermont, but by then their relationship was already unstable. Other students took note of how aggressive Holmes acted toward Clara, but she didn't stand for this very long. She uprooted herself and her child in 1884 and moved back to New Hampshire, never to hear from Holmes again.

Holmes transferred to the University of Michigan in Ann Arbor, which was known for its programs in the medical field. Many speculate that this was where Holmes found his love for death, as several of his fellow students noted his obsession with human dissection. He was always eager to explain the gory details of his work and sometimes took the cadavers home for his personal use.

Soon, he turned morbidly creative in his pursuits. Holmes began swindling insurance companies for money, going to elaborate lengths to take out fraudulent insurance policies. He would disfigure stolen cadavers and restage their deaths to look like accidents; this ensured that each victim's beneficiary (who always happened to be Holmes) would receive the maximum settlement. The insurance money would end up in his pocket and he would do it all over again.

In his early adulthood, Holmes continued to commit fraud and other schemes against anyone who fell for his faux charisma. He moved across the country from city to city for years to avoid paying bills and continuously increased his personal wealth, hardly ever paying a cent for anything. By 1886, he had finally landed in Chicago, a city budding with opportunity, and decided to pursue a new life under the pseudonym H. H. Holmes. Some want to believe he chose the name, dramatically, of course, to honor Arthur Conan Doyle's famous detective, Sherlock Holmes, but the first story to star the sleuth wasn't published until a year later. The truth is it might have been just another one of his aliases, randomly chosen only to end up famously haunting the headlines years later.

After arriving in Chicago, Holmes settled in the Englewood neighborhood, where he took up a job as a drugstore clerk. The place was owned by a Dr. Elizabeth S. Holton, who welcomed Holmes's offer to help out around the store. He was just the person she could use to man the ground floor while she ran the everyday operations. While many stories portray Dr. Holton as an elderly woman with a bedridden husband, they were actually young adults not much older than Holmes. They also shared an alma mater, which meant that Holmes seeking out the store was probably not a coincidence. Proven to be hardworking, Holmes eventually purchased the drugstore from Dr. Holton and she and her husband moved out of the building. Paying Dr. Holton for the property was one of the few times that Holmes actually followed through on his word, as he usually wiggled his way out of spending a dime on anything. No one knows how Dr. Holton was able to ensure Holmes paid what he owed, but perhaps he counted the remittance worth his first step toward a much grander scheme.

Holmes started to run a relatively successful business in Dr. Holton's absence, but he wanted more than just a drugstore.

He bought a section of property across the street, at 63rd and Wallace, and started forming plans for a very unique building. Not only would his property offer a pharmacy, a jewelry store, and upstairs apartments, but he was also cultivating ideas for something secret and unique. Holmes wanted total freedom in his own home to pull off crimes more wicked than his previous misdeeds. Roughly three and a half miles away from Jackson Park, where the world's fair would draw thousands of visitors to the city just six years later, Holmes built a covert labyrinth to carry out his baleful intentions.

Around the same time, Myrta Belknap, a young lady Holmes knew from his past, stumbled back into his life. They were married in 1887 while he was still legally wed to his first wife, Clara. Holmes was exceptionally charming, even attractive, with a bushy mustache and frosty eyes that Myrta found captivating. So when she came to work for Holmes in his drugstore and found that many other women also recognized his allure, she grew jealous of their flirting and confronted her husband about it. Holmes's solution was to assign her the task of bookkeeping, which kept her upstairs and away from the storefront, as if he was clearing an unwanted object from his path to success.

Myrta wasn't going to comply with his poor problem-solving, so she left to live with her parents up in Wilmette, Illinois, where she raised Lucy, her first child with Holmes. He would bring them cash and gifts when he came to visit. As time passed, however, those visits became increasingly infrequent as he spent more time obsessing over his new building and what he would do with it.

Murder Castle was a yearlong project that took up the entire city block and was built by many changing hands so that no one knew the full extent of Holmes's diabolical planning. He hired his workers on contract but rarely ever paid them. When men came asking for a paycheck after completing their contracted work, Holmes would tell them they had delivered poor results and fire them instead. His penny-pinching habits helped him save money and keep the intention of Murder Castle a secret to all those involved, though many still noticed his suspicious behavior.

Holmes's malicious building was finished far before the world's fair opened on May 1, 1893, and took many victims before he started using the upstairs apartments to quarter hotel guests. His very own version of hell was complete and ready for lost souls to wander into it. For all the work he put into creating the ominously intricate castle, Holmes was nothing short of a genius. Unfortunately, he was also a madman.

The Columbian Exposition attracted over twenty-seven million visitors to Chicago despite the limited transportation methods of the era. Plenty of travelers couldn't afford to stay in Chicago's high-end hotels, but lodgings at Holmes's hotel were cheap. Business was booming and Holmes needed employees to help him operate the hotel. In addition to running newspaper ads that advertised his building, Holmes attended the world's fair himself, primarily to seek out young women journeying to the Windy City for the first time, many of whom were hungry for the endless opportunities that Chicago could offer. Eager to find their start in the working world, these women sought shelter in Holmes's sinister sanctuary for the convenience of having their lodgings and employment in the same building.

Holmes's employees noticed that the hotel had a high turnover rate. People frequently disappeared after starting work at the drugstore, and though suspicion existed among the staff, many assumed the best-case scenario rather than take action in case of the worst. No one ever reported their notions to authorities or confronted Holmes, and his near decade in Chicago passed without a single run-in with police. Operating undetected for years, Holmes committed horrific and unforgivable acts in Murder Castle.

Holmes didn't choose his victims at random. He killed because he believed he had exhausted the use of that particular person and they would henceforth be a bother to him or otherwise useless. Holmes's murders were obviously premeditated, his telltale sign being that he always asked his victims to take out life insurance policies with him designated as the beneficiary. With their full trust in Holmes, these people fell for his schemes, allowed him to steal from them in death, and one by one vanished from the city.

Once Holmes was set on getting rid of someone in his way, there was nothing to stop the series of torments that followed. He never disposed of them quickly, instead utilizing the complex designs of Murder Castle to torture and maim them before delivering an excruciating death. None of his victims saw any mercy before the light left their eyes. Holmes enjoyed the slow slaughter.

Most of Holmes's victims were pretty young bachelorettes, but his first official slaying in Murder Castle was his mistress. In early 1890, Ned Connor moved into one of

Holmes's upstairs apartments with his wife, Julia, and their daughter, Pearl. He got a job managing the jewelry counter at the drugstore downstairs, so Julia also took up a job at the drugstore. Noticing her immediately, Holmes began flirting with her in public while on the clock; it didn't take long before Ned grew angry with both of them. Ned and Julia divorced, leaving Pearl in her mother's custody and both alone with Holmes.

Julia started to get involved in all of Holmes's small businesses, paying him installments over time to become part owner in the drugstore and other endeavors. This was one of Holmes's tactics: to set up an easy payment plan and suggest his employees write notes to him so they could gain more stock in the business. Julia enjoyed Holmes's attention and appreciated the opportunity that she thought would bring her more wealth in the future. In an effort to impress Holmes or perhaps to find autonomy to care for her child, Julia continued to sign checks over to Holmes as their relationship progressed.

Pulling scams was Holmes's original pony trick, and he wasn't about to actually let Julia profit from his businesses. After spending a few months with friends during which she made no mention of traveling anytime soon, Julia and Pearl went missing. They were last seen on Christmas Eve 1891, two more victims fallen prey to Murder Castle.

Chatter spread around the drugstore, but Holmes quieted the whispers by explaining that Julia had gone out of town. Then he hired a man named Charles M. Chapel to perform a very specific task. Holmes paid the man $36 to tear the flesh off of a cadaver and reassemble the skeleton for display. Chapel assumed that the body was from one of Holmes's patients and the morbid request was purely for medical-related research purposes. Holmes sold the skeleton to Hahnemann Medical College in Chicago for quite a bit of money; authentic donations were rare at the time and universities were desperate for research tools. This became Holmes's preferred method of hiding the bodies of his murder victims. Chapel continued to work for Holmes, all the time not knowing—or, rather, pretending not to know—that he was an accomplice to one of the most sinister villains who ever descended upon the city.

During his time in the Windy City, Holmes took on another accomplice, Benjamin Pitezel, who knew only some of Murder Castle's secrets. Pitezel had a criminal history and, after finding kinship with Holmes, became his tool in committing several offenses. Most notably, he helped perpetuate a financial scheme with Holmes, victimizing Minnie Williams, an amateur actress who moved to Chicago in 1893. Minnie fell hard for Holmes and accepted a job as his personal stenographer so that they could spend more time together. She was so eager to start a life with him that she even signed over her affluent property in Fort Worth, Texas, to one of Holmes's aliases, Alexander Bond. Holmes later transferred the deed to one of Pitezel's false names and moved Minnie to an apartment in Lincoln Park. When her sister Nannie came to visit that July, the two fell prey to Holmes's fatal schemes. The last time their family heard from them was through a letter from Nannie, though possibly written by Holmes himself, claiming they had left on a trip to Europe.

No one ever accused Holmes of murder, even though several families of his victims grew concerned when their loved ones stopped writing. Holmes targeted wealthy women, usually coaxing them into giving up their fortunes with the promise of marriage before sending them to their fate. Since these women usually wrote home to fawn over their wonderful new fiancé, many families weren't suspicious that Holmes inherited their wealth when they suddenly disappeared. Family members were often forced to believe that their loved ones were involved in some kind of accident, never suspecting Holmes.

Instead, it was Holmes's debts that would lead to his eventual capture. Creditors started looking into Holmes's accounts and realized that he had never made a payment on his building, which finally put Holmes in the hot seat. He worked under this pressure for a few more months, but by 1894, he had little reason to stay in Chicago.

When Holmes left Chicago, he took Pitezel with him, but only after insuring his life for $10,000. Pitezel knew about the insurance policy, as Holmes had told him they would fake his death to collect the money, a long con they wouldn't carry out for a while. They ended up in Fort Worth, Texas, where Holmes started up another drugstore business, hoping to build a second and even more intricate Murder Castle and continue his wicked work. He intended to pull the same scheme as before, attempting to fool suppliers into letting him buy goods on credit without ever paying them back. But this time, Holmes was caught.

Located on modern-day Commerce and Second Streets, the Fort Worth drugstore was part of the deal Holmes had swindled from the Williams sisters. But when he tried to ship mortgaged goods to St. Louis, Missouri, particularly a string of horses, Holmes was arrested for fraud in July 1894. Holmes spent only a few months in jail, during which he met a train robber named Marion Hedgepeth. Holmes promised Hedgepeth $500 for the name of a shady attorney who could free him of his charges. To gain the other man's trust, Holmes confided in Hedgepeth about the scheme he would pull once he left jail: faking Ben Pitezel's death and collecting the insurance money. Hedgepeth agreed to help Holmes, and the serial murderer walked out of jail.

Holmes's and Pitezel's plan was to use a disfigured cadaver and stage an explosion in Pitezel's new office. He owned his own business under an alias, B. F. Perry, so it would have been an easy getaway. But Pitezel was ignorant; his accomplice was a murderer, after all, not just a scammer. Instead of faking a death, Holmes pulled off the actual murder of Ben Pitezel by knocking him out with chloroform and setting him on fire. He then orchestrated the explosion and made a run for it with the blood money.

Insurance companies looked into Pitezel's false identity, not realizing it was an alias, and were unable to find any surviving family. They eventually received a letter regarding B. F. Perry's accounts, which named Ben Pitezel as the actual owner. Growing suspicious of the incident, they reported this to the police, who began an investigation into the death. Holmes might have gotten away with murder one more time if not for his sloppy work in jail. He had never paid Hedgepeth. Angry that he had never received his $500 referral fee, Hedgepeth snitched on Holmes to the police, which alerted them to the scheme Holmes already had well underway.

During this time, Holmes fled to Boston to live with Pitezel's wife and children, to whom he never paid a single dime of Ben's insurance money. As the pressure built, Holmes decided that it was time he murdered three of Pitezel's children to make sure they didn't give him up. But the good guys were already closing in on Holmes and these innocents died for nothing.

The Pinkerton Detective Agency, a firm notable for its claims to have stopped an early assassination attempt against Abraham Lincoln, was brought onto Holmes's insurance case. Its agents quickly tracked Holmes down and arrested him in Boston. He was taken in for questioning on November 17, 1894, on accusations of fraud.

The battle for Holmes's confession was arduous. It took almost a year, until the summer of 1895, before Holmes pled guilty to just one count of insurance fraud, but what was exposed during the trial eventually sealed his fate. A stubborn criminal who refused to be caught, Holmes made up so many lies about his insurance scheme that he was unable to tell the truth anymore and constantly misspoke. He certainly couldn't answer any questions about where Pitezel was, and detectives eventually realized that Holmes may have been involved in his death, a case they were investigating separately. After detectives found the bodies of the Pitezel children, they began an investigation into Holmes's ominous building back in Englewood.

When Chicago police searched Murder Castle, they were horrified. Human remains littered the basement, found in stoves, fireplaces, chimneys, and the kiln, which also contained bone fragments even of a small child. Surgical instruments were founded bloodied and blunted on dissecting tables, and a vat of corrosive acid lurked, bubbling, in the shadows. No one will ever know the exact number of people Holmes killed because a fire cut the investigation short, sweeping up the remaining evidence of Murder Castle in August 1895.

Once the window of truth was cracked open just a bit, everything was suddenly flooded with light. Perhaps knowing he was already a dead man or because he wanted to take credit for his hard work, Holmes held nothing back. Rather than try to defend himself anymore, he bragged about his killings, professing to have claimed over two hundred lives during the course of the Columbian Exposition and afterward. Historians still debate the actual number of his victims, though he was ultimately tried for twenty-seven murders.

While awaiting trial, Holmes wrote a short autobiography titled *Holmes's Own Story.* "I was born with the devil in me," he wrote. "I could not help the fact that I was a murderer, no more than the poet can help the inspiration to sing . . . I was born with the 'Evil One' standing as my sponsor beside the bed where I was ushered into the world, and he has been with me since."

Holmes was tried in Philadelphia for the murder of Benjamin Pitezel, among many others, and sentenced to death by hanging. His official execution took place on May 7, 1896.

His neck did not snap mercifully; there was no killing him instantly. Instead, H. H. Holmes writhed and choked to death slowly until he was pronounced dead as night twenty minutes later.

Chapter Two

The Everleigh Club

The Lavish Brothel in Chicago's Red-Light District

Vice has always plagued the streets of Chicago in some form or another, but the pinnacle of its bad reputation in the early twentieth century primarily crept up from the Levee, the city's very own red-light district. This vice-heavy region of Chicago was attractive to the greedy, and it made the perfect market for shady business opportunities. Locals today know the area as the South Loop, but at its zenith, this lakeside community was filled to the brim with brothels, saloons, dance halls, and, most of all, the illustrious Everleigh Club.

The Levee District was a sweeping section of the south end of the Loop dedicated only to nightly entertainment and operated beneath the eyes of the law from 1880 to 1912. The most likely frequenters of the Levee District were power-hungry men, who stumbled down there well past midnight to indulge in illegal gambling and mob dealings and to drunkenly splurge on a lady of the night. But women were not empowered by their work, and they received very little pay for long nights of catering to multiple sexual partners. However much it took a toll on their bodies, women found that sex work was one of the few occupations they could count on to remain reliable, at least while they were still young.

The aldermen in that district were crooked to the core; Michael "Hinky Dink" Kenna and "Bathhouse" John Coughlin often held political fundraisers that attracted a mingling of the most notorious Chicago figures, including gangsters, politicians, police captains, and sex workers. These two aldermen made friends with the nefarious to enhance their personal wealth, even letting slide the notorious success of the Everleigh Club.

Dubbed the most prestigious brothel in Chicago during the unbridled reign of the Levee District, the Everleigh Club was owned and operated by two sisters, Ada and Minna Simms. Two years apart in age and exceptional business partners, Ada and Minna didn't get their start in the Second City, but they certainly made a name for themselves by the time they left.

Ada and Minna adopted the Everleigh last name from a habit of their grandmother, who used to end letters with "Everly Yours." These Southern belles from Greene County, Virginia, were given a fine education, capitalizing on their natural street smarts to become truly brilliant young women. The sisters both married early in life but divorced under unknown circumstances. With the road open to endless possibility, they made the trek to Omaha, Nebraska, where they opened their very first brothel together in 1895.

Their initial endeavor was majorly successful, mostly due to the draw that Ada and Minna brought to the city. Men were fascinated with the idea of sister madams and assumed the girls waiting inside the brothel were that much more enthralling. They charged a steep $10 entry fee, a payment the average man couldn't just make on a whim. Only the proudest men flaunted their wealth by happily paying the expensive admission, which only made Ada and Minna more affluent.

Thanks to the influx of tourists for the Trans-Mississippi and International Exposition of 1898, the sisters doubled their investment when they opened a second brothel closer to the venue. And, while their revenue would have certainly increased over time had they stayed in Nebraska, the sisters decided to close the doors in 1899 and take their business to a more lucrative and popular city. Besides, they had just raked in about $70,000, equivalent to over $2.1 million in 2020. And they weren't ready to slow down yet. The sisters moved to Chicago that same year, ready to take on the business venture of a lifetime.

That's not the story they told everyone, though. Years later, when the Everleigh Club was in full swing, Ada and Minna gave patrons a more mysterious backstory that included abusive marriages to two brothers, followed by a sudden rise to fame as actresses, and then a claim to a hefty inheritance from their deceased father. The sisters may have been trying to protect themselves and their true name or just desired to enhance their mystique around town; either way, the false stories made them all the more interesting.

Regardless of how they ended up in Chicago in 1899, it was perfect timing for the mischievous sisters. One of the few booming industries where two young women could actually find jobs in that era was sex work, but Ada and Minna Everleigh had much grander plans. They were already well-versed enough with their previous business experience, and the Chicago market was hungry for new places to frequent.

On February 1, 1900, the Everleigh Club opened for business in the Levee District of Chicago, forever changing the history of the city's red-light district. On opening night, Minna Everleigh turned away the first group of guests that came to visit, knowing exactly what she was doing. Disgruntled, the men fled to local bars and complained loudly about the new club that wasn't accepting patrons on its first night in business. Sure enough, a wealthier and more prestigious clientele came knocking on the front door and, flashing their wallets at Minna, were promptly led inside.

Located at 2131 South Dearborn, the Everleigh Club was a shining gem on the dark street. The $50 admission fee to this fifty-room mansion made every other brothel pale in comparison, even if it was far more expensive than a night anywhere else. In 1902, the Everleigh sisters expanded the club to include the neighboring building, 2133 South Dearborn Street, calling this extra space the Annex.

Opulent parlors awaited each guest who waltzed through the door, self-possessed enough to pay their fees to the most exclusive brothel in the city. That was the Everleigh secret, after all: make them feel like they couldn't afford to be here anyway, and they will flock. These men had everything to prove, and they weren't going to soil their reputations at some lower-level club. The Everleigh Club was the only brothel in town about which a man could proudly boast his visit.

Among the parlors were the Gold Room, the Chinese Room, the Persian Room, the Japanese Throne Room, the Turkish Room, the Rose Parlor, the Silver Parlor, and the Room of a Thousand Mirrors. Silk curtains draped every room, while impressive oriental rugs parted the golden sea of damask easy chairs and hardwood floors. Gold-rimmed china and silver dinnerware dressed the mahogany tables, while perfumed fountains showered lovely musks all over the rooms. A $15,000 gold-leafed piano graced the Music Room, and mirrored ceilings gave the scenes unfolding beneath them a grander perspective. The Everleigh Club housed a fully furnished library with finely bound books and nude paintings covering every wall of its art gallery. Hostesses wove in and out of the rooms, catering to every need their guests might have, constantly playing to their emotions and physical desires to coax more money out of the gentlemen. The Everleigh sisters saw to it that a four-piece orchestra was always playing at the prestigious club.

Prices at the Everleigh Club were of colossal proportions compared to their rivals: champagne was $12 in the parlor and $15 in the rooms, and dinners cost $50 per person without the company of a lady. The meal alone equates to about $1,500 in 2020, a complete and undeniable luxury, surpassing even the most prestigious restaurants in Chicago today. Time with one of the Everleigh butterflies cost an extra $50, and those who didn't spend at least that much were turned away the next time around. They clearly couldn't afford a stay with one of the Everleigh's cherished courtesans.

The draw of the Everleigh Club came from the attentiveness of the women inside. The sex workers there provided their customers with an experience, flirting lengthily with them and allowing each man to pursue them over the course of the night. They gave their clients their undivided attention, perpetuating the illusion that they genuinely cared about what these men thought and said, even if just for a night. Ada and Minna realized that, more than sex, men really just wanted to feel a little less alone. And they capitalized massively on fulfilling that need, often making over $5,000 in a single night ($153,000 in 2020).

The Everleigh sisters referred to their employees as "butterflies," and the standards were exceptionally high. They had to audition, but first they had to have a pretty face and figure, be in perfect health, and look well in evening clothes, according to an ad placed for employment. Butterflies were to be graceful, well-read, and conversational, in addition to performing a range of sex acts. Consent was important to the sisters and the girls were required to be eighteen years or older, undergo doctor's exams, and refuse drug usage. The courtesans employed at the Everleigh Club usually didn't mind these high standards, however, because they were paid far better than they ever dreamt they would be. They raked in anywhere from $100 to $400 a week, the latter amount equating to roughly $12,200 in 2020, which means these women made about a $600,000 annual salary in today's terms. They also never entertained more than a few men per night. In Minna's words, "One $50 client is preferable to ten $5 ones. Less wear and tear."

Celebrities known to frequent the Everleigh Club included business owner Marshall Field Jr., poet Edgar Lee Masters, author Theodore Dreiser, columnist Ring Lardner, industrialist John Warne Gates, boxer Jack Johnson, actor John Barrymore, and, of course, aldermen "Hinky Dink" Kenna and "Bathhouse" Coughlin. They were both instantly captivated by the Everleigh sisters' opulent flair and enjoyed themselves deeply every time they came around. Ada and Minna knew how to play this game. The sisters coaxed the aldermen's egos, cleverly making sure they always heard their praise from other people, until the men were quite fond of Ada and Minna. All at once, the Everleigh sisters had gained two powerful allies and were even invited to the city's most infamous party, the First Ward Ball of 1901.

Held every year since 1896 by the crooked aldermen, the ball was Chicago's filthiest display of open sin. The city's most notorious, yet powerful and often political, characters gathered together for a single night to self-indulge for hours with the Levee District's sex workers. Kenna and Coughlin went to every madam in the red-light district and strongly encouraged them to purchase tickets for their courtesans, so that there would be plenty in attendance at the event.

Ada and Minna needed to impress their new political acquaintances, so they took the opportunity to present their most beautiful courtesans to the party. Dressed in the finest threads, laced with diamonds and ready to enthrall, the Everleigh butterflies certainly made an imposing presence before the public that night. In a grand gesture of alliance, Coughlin was escorted into the party with an Everleigh sister on each arm.

In 1902, the Everleigh Club saw its most famous visitor: Prince Heinrich of Prussia, the brother of German kaiser Wilhelm II. The sisters made elaborate plans to impress his company, sparing no detail when it came to the quality of the food, drink, and entertainment. They held a dance performance in his honor, and during the show, one of the dancer's shoes flung from her foot, knocking over a bottle of champagne, which poured into the sole. Out of chivalry to the lady, one of Heinrich's men drank the champagne from the shoe to spare her a wet heel, a gesture that is thought to have inspired a similarly odd party tradition in today's culture.

There seemed to be nothing that could bring down the Everleigh Club, but bloodshed almost did the trick. A young Marshall Field Jr., heir to the Marshall Field and Company empire, visited the Everleigh Club with a date, Vera Scott, on November 22, 1905, and not for the first time. Upon arrival, they were escorted to a room with a butterfly. Whatever Field's intentions were, he was being overly forward when Vera grabbed his gun, pointed it at him, and told him to stand down. But the hair trigger on the pistol was all that was needed to accidentally shoot her date, one who happened to be a massive public figure. They bundled Field into a cab and took him home, where he claimed that he accidentally shot himself and was found by his servants. His father paid Vera and the sex worker to keep quiet about the truth, but when he died a few days later, the scandal only grew more elaborate.

Ada and Minna were nearly framed for the murder of Field Jr. by a competing brothel madam, who was jealous of the Everleigh Club's success. Madam Vic Shaw enlisted the first black brothel owner in Chicago, Pony Moore, to concoct a scheme to take down Minna for the murder, but the plan fizzled out when they tried to involve the butterflies. Minna found out about the already failing plans when one of her courtesans let her in on the secret. Minna even brought a Chicago cop with her to confront the brothel madams. No one was arrested for the scheme, however. Framing someone for murder was apparently just typical Levee District behavior, according to authorities.

The Everleigh sisters' success came to an abrupt halt on October 24, 1911, when Mayor Carter Harrison Jr. heard of a report that claimed there were six hundred brothels in Chicago. He was in the middle of a campaign that prided itself on trying to restore dignity to Chicago and he wouldn't have this news soiling his reputation. After reading an official advertisement for the Everleigh Club, one created and distributed by Ada Everleigh herself, he immediately ordered the club shuttered. The sisters had previously avoided being closed down by bribing city aldermen when it came to legal matters, but they were content to close their doors without a fuss.

Minna and Ada Everleigh left Chicago with over $1 million in cash, jewelry, stocks, and bonds, equivalent to no less than $27 million in 2020. By the end of their eleven-year run, the Everleigh Club was the most famous brothel in America.

"If it weren't for married men, we couldn't have carried on at all," Minna famously said, following the news of the brothel closing. "And if it weren't for cheating married women, we could have made another million."

CHAPTER THREE

Al Capone

Chicago's Most Glorified Criminal

CHICAGO TOURISM HAS CAPITALIZED ON THE AL CAPONE mania, plastering his fat, scarred face upon every shot glass, fridge magnet, and postcard you can pick up at O'Hare International Airport. Scarface never left the hearts of Chicagoans, even decades after his tragically drawn-out death. Capone was known for killing dozens of people and ordering the deaths of countless others, but he also supplied bootlegged alcohol at the time of Prohibition, making him a beloved hero in the public eye. We still romanticize Capone's criminal background, almost worshipping the idea of a villain able to evade the law and provide alcohol to the thirsty, but perhaps it isn't too far removed or less deserved. Capone was a public servant in his early years; he established a shelter for the homeless and gave back to those in need during the bitter Chicago winters. He made a positive difference in the neighborhoods neglected by those in power, and the community saw him as an ally.

Even though Al Capone is undoubtedly esteemed, there's no denying his ruthless and untamed behavior. The majority of his violence was directed toward other gangsters, and Capone was intensely brutal, sometimes having those who double-crossed him clobbered to death with baseball bats before mercifully firing bullets into their skulls to end it all. Sometimes Capone got his hands dirty, but for the most part, he ordered his cronies to carry out these violent acts while he watched.

He was constantly dodging the law, routinely targeted and arrested by the police only to be released for lack of evidence connecting him to the crime. He enjoyed participating in press interviews that followed and seemed to milk his celebrity for all it was worth. Above it all, he believed he wasn't doing anything wrong; as he put it, the majority of Chicagoans were already indulging in these practices and he was just providing a service. But Capone was not innocent, as history has shown.

In the end, even after all of his murderous involvement, it wasn't the killings that sent him to prison. Out of all the crimes Capone committed in his life, tax evasion was his ultimate undoing. It only goes to show that when money is involved, people will go to extensive lengths to bring that money home.

Leaving a paper trail as a criminal is not the smartest route to take, but Al Capone was otherwise an extremely wily and intelligent person. Born to Italian immigrant parents in Brooklyn, New York, at the beginning of 1899, Capone was immediately immersed in the crime world. He was initiated into a small street gang after dropping out of the sixth grade and he worked his way up the ladder. At the invite of mob boss Johnny Torrio, who heard that Capone was quickly becoming a viable asset, Capone moved to Chicago when he was twenty years old and picked up a job as a bouncer at a brothel. Capone also got involved in some legitimate business in the cleaning and dyeing field, which gained him a favorable reputation among public officials, labor unions, and employees' associations. A hero to the homeless, Capone always gave back to those in poverty, fulfilling the needs that the city's people in power often neglected and supplying the celebratory booze everyone craved. He was a Robin Hood to this city.

Capone's first experience in Chicago's organized crime scene was working under Torrio as part of a larger network of underworld criminals held up by crime boss James "Big Jim" Colosimo. A major disagreement occurred between Torrio and Colosimo just after Capone arrived, which led to some changes in the Chicago Outfit. While the gang was initially profitable through the exploitation of sex workers, Torrio was convinced they could make a lot more money bootlegging alcohol, since Prohibition had just been rolled out that January, 1920. Colosimo refused to put his men at further risk, though. Alcohol could get them into a lot of trouble and he wasn't willing to compromise the scheme they had going just to be greedy. Torrio had other plans that would put him on top.

That May, Colosimo was gunned down while waiting for a shipment of stolen goods at one of the restaurants he owned. When the delivery, supposedly organized by Torrio, didn't make it on time, Colosimo stepped outside to figure out what was going on, just as gang member Frankie Yale was walking up. The two apparently exchanged some words before Yale shot Colosimo in cold blood. Torrio's message had been delivered loud and clear.

The ruthless Torrio took over Colosimo's position in the gang and made sure Capone took up his old job as right-hand man. Together, they got involved in the bootlegging industry, taking on the business of distilling and distributing prohibited alcohol by the time Capone was twenty-one years old. They were finally raking in their preferred level of dough, but they had some competition, primarily with the North Side Irish Gang run by Charles Dean O'Banion, and eventually, George "Bugs" Moran. Over the next decade, the Italians and the Irish initiated small turf wars that caused death all over the city.

The bullets were bad for business, though, as average citizens were wary of buying alcohol in shady neighborhoods for fear of getting shot. Torrio and O'Banion tried to come to an agreement in 1921, that the Italians ruled the South Side and the Irish ruled the North Side. They went into business together in several industries to ensure that if they ever turned against each other, they would be sacrificing a lot of money.

But then a West Side gang popped up, the Terrible Gennas, who were also Italian but separate from the Chicago Outfit. When they attempted to expand their territory into the North Side, irritating O'Banion, Torrio tried to smooth things over between his new allies. O'Banion was stubborn, though, and refused to forgive the Gennas for their territorial robbery. Torrio enlisted Capone that year to persuade the Irish another way, intending to break their fragile truce.

They called upon Frankie Yale once again, who gunned down O'Banion in his Schofield Flower Shop in November 1924. Yale was never charged for these high-profile murders, the deeds carefully muddled by his fellow gang members so that no one really knew how the gang committed these crimes. Moran took O'Banion's place in the Irish Mob, and his own bloody reign of terror began. Capone and Moran were bitter rivals over the years and they eventually forced Torrio out. In 1925, when Torrio was brutally injured in a shootout orchestrated by Moran, the Mafia head fled Chicago and spent his remaining years in Italy, unaffiliated with the criminal life. Torrio left the big boss spot up to Capone, who eagerly claimed his title among the Italian Mafia.

By the time the Roaring Twenties were in full swing, Capone's notorious Chicago Outfit was the leading crime organization in the city, specializing in prostitution, gambling, and bootlegging alcohol during Prohibition. While everyone around him was partying their wealth away, Capone was furtively collecting all the revenue for alcohol sales behind the scenes. Under Capone, the Chicago Outfit raked in as much as $105 million annually—approximately $2.8 billion in 2020—primarily through bootlegging. This meant that Capone maintained a net worth of over $100 million at the time ($2.7 billion in 2020), making him one of the world's wealthiest gangsters. That was definitely enough to get the press interested in Capone's comings and goings. They dubbed him Scarface, a nickname he detested, for the three indelible marks that raked across his face. Although he wrote them off as battle wounds, he was never involved in the military; he got them in a bar fight when he was seventeen, for insulting a woman.

Capone and Moran were in constant battle with each other, but the most famous altercation by far was the St. Valentine's Day Massacre. At the height of tension between the rival gangs in 1929, Capone's men, disguised as police officers, visited a North Side garage at 2122 North Clark Street in Lincoln Park on Valentine's Day. Moran ran his bootlegging operation there, and his crew was not expecting the brutal attack that ensued. Seven men were caught unaware when the phony officers arrived and pretended to arrest them, lining them up against a wall and gunning them down mercilessly.

Moran escaped by a hair; he was running late and had nearly pulled up to the garage when he spotted a police vehicle outside. Assuming it was a regular police shakedown, Moran decided to wait it out and meet his men later, stepping into a coffee shop in the meantime. When he realized what had really happened, Moran fled the carnage. He later raged to the press, condemning the Italian Mafia for the murders: "Only Capone kills guys like that."

Chicago police showed up later to find only one man still alive: Frank Gusenberg. They rushed him to Alexian Brothers Hospital, but he was barely clinging to life. Police sergeant Clarence Sweeney pressed him for information, begging him to reveal what happened at the garage that day, but he wouldn't talk. He died from his wounds later that night.

Since Moran had named Capone, police contacted him and requested an alibi, but his story was straight. Capone was taking a vacation at his Florida home, more than a thousand miles away, but he offered his own opinion on the murders to the press. "The only man who kills like that," he said, "is Bugs Moran."

Capone was never tried in conjunction with the massacre, but there was a fair amount of evidence to suggest that he was the man behind the scenes. After all, Moran was a longtime enemy of Scarface, and the Italian and Irish gang tensions only made it that much worse. Arrests were made on both sides of the gang war, but in the end, no one was tried for the murders. One thing was certain, though. No one was about to question Capone's reign over the criminal underworld after that.

Public sentiment regarding Capone tanked, however, as Chicagoans realized how severe this criminal truly was. They demanded reform that included putting Capone behind bars, but no one wanted to wait for the feds to catch up with the mobster. The Italian Mafia in New York stepped in with a secret setup to arrest Capone and get him off the streets for a while. Capone traveled to Philadelphia in May 1929, where his arrest for concealed carry was arranged and executed. He was sentenced to a year in the Eastern State Penitentiary, just as planned, but released on good behavior after only ten months. Just a week after he left prison in March 1930, Al Capone was named the very first Public Enemy Number One by the Chicago Crime Commission.

In February 1931, Capone was arrested again for contempt charges and brought to Cook County Jail, originally just for six months. Meanwhile, the US Treasury Department launched a full investigation into Capone's monetary affairs with an inkling that something was off about the man's massive income. Not only was he bootlegging, promoting prostitution, and running a gambling business, but he was also evading income tax, an oversight that finally put him behind bars. After all the trouble that Al Capone had put the Chicago police force through, he was finally going to be locked up for good.

Capone was indicted for evasion of federal income tax and convicted that October. He was sentenced to eleven years in Atlanta, and then Alcatraz, but ended up serving only eight. This was, in part, due to the onset of syphilis, a debilitating disease that spread from his genitals to his brain over the course of a few months.

In November 1939, Capone was released from Alcatraz prison. He had paid off all of his fines and back taxes, and every money-related crime he had committed had been resolved. By the end of his life in prison, his syphilis was causing brain damage and it's possible he had little recollection of his crimes in his final moments.

He was immediately brought to Baltimore Hospital following his release but no one on the premises wanted to admit him, strictly due to his dreadful reputation. He was then brought to his Palm Island, Florida, home, where he lived out the remainder of his life with the mental capacity of a twelve-year-old boy. A stroke and pneumonia eventually took his life on January 25, 1947.

Al Capone never publicly returned to Chicago, but he made his final resting place a garden for the criminally fascinated. He was buried at Mount Carmel Catholic Cemetery in Hillside, Illinois, a very large and ceremonious gravesite that resides far from the restless urban streets.

CHAPTER FOUR

John Dillinger

Gunshots at Biograph Theater

THE GANGSTER ERA SPAWNED AN ENTIRE BREED OF CRIMI-
nals who were simultaneously despised by the feds and
adored by the common folk. Their portrayal in the media
reminds you of legends of old—immortalized and misun-
derstood Robin Hood–like figures who taunted the wealthy
and gave back to the community. John Dillinger was one of
these outlaw heroes, and his crimes were continuously mis-
interpreted by the media, which praised his cunning over the
greed of American banks.

Dillinger was a handsome young bank robber with an
unmistakable glimmer of mischief twinkling in each eye. He
wandered roguishly across America, finding his way back
to Chicago again and again throughout his criminal career.
He built an infamous reputation that far exceeded any other
gangster before him, and his habit of avoiding capture by
just a hair won him the favor of the American public. Leaving a trail of death and loss in his wake, Dillinger had a bad

boy reputation and always did more harm than good, but his only concern was getting away clean.

An Indianapolis man born and raised, Dillinger was cheeky, so he often found himself in trouble. The criminal life had always appealed to Dillinger, who joined a young neighborhood gang called the Dirty Dozen to engage in petty crimes like theft and trespassing. He eventually led other boys in terrorizing kids at school, including a young girl he had group-raped when he was just thirteen years old. He dropped out of high school in 1919.

Noticing a pattern in John's behavior that would lead to worse habits down the road, his father moved the family from the big city to a small farm in Mooresville, Indiana, hoping the quiet life would help settle down his son. The move had the opposite effect on the young criminal, however. The city had its teeth in him and all Dillinger wanted to do was get out of town.

He decided to enlist in the navy, out of civic duty or perhaps seeking adventure. Whatever it was, he didn't last long. Dillinger abandoned the USS *Utah* just a few months after joining in 1923. Bravery comes in many forms, but desertion is hardly one of them. Dillinger was later dishonorably discharged.

Many historians consider this a turning point for Dillinger. After leaving the navy, Dillinger settled down with a seventeen-year-old girl named Beryl Ethel Hovious in Martinsville, Indiana, and unbeknownst to her, the young man began committing minor burglaries around town. The criminal in him took hold of his destiny with an iron grip and it never let go.

After being caught in a failed holdup at a Mooresville grocery store on September 6, 1924, Dillinger was sentenced to a decade in prison and ended up wasting the next eight and a half years, almost a third of his life, behind bars at the Indiana State Reformatory at Pendleton. When his wife divorced him in 1929 and he was denied parole, Dillinger grew extremely bitter about his situation. He tried to escape a number of times and was accused of being disorderly. He positively hated incarceration.

Dillinger learned the art of bank robbery through the inmates serving time with him at Pendleton. Several criminals incarcerated there had also made escape attempts and had pulled off intricate bank heists Dillinger admired. He picked up tricks of the trade and realized where he had gone wrong before. Dillinger vowed he would never again be caught. He eventually played the prison boards by feigning good behavior, a move that stopped him from receiving extra time on his sentence. When Dillinger was officially released on parole on May 22, 1933, he put his newfound knowledge to the test almost immediately.

Along with a few other partners in crime, many of whom he had met in prison, Dillinger embarked on a bank-robbing spree, holding up and shooting up five establishments across Indiana and Ohio within the next four months. The Pinkerton Detective Agency, the very same that had caught H. H. Holmes three decades earlier, was sent after Dillinger, but he always avoided capture with moments to spare. The press went wild, exalting Dillinger's theatrical behavior and falsely romanticizing his personhood, and the American public instantly fell in love with the idea of this dapper criminal.

This ego inflation could have only fueled the fire that Dillinger was spreading. He was entirely in his element, cool as ice and seemingly couldn't be stopped. But with such a recognizable and handsome face, it was only a matter of time before the debonair gunman was found.

While visiting an old flame in Dayton, Ohio, Dillinger found himself in a brawl with her ex-husband. The assault itself could have gotten him arrested, but when he fled the scene, he left behind his hat and a fountain pen engraved with his name. Pinkerton detectives were already on the lookout for the infamous criminal, and when Dillinger was seen a few months later at his ex-girlfriend's house, they finally nabbed him. Dillinger was jailed at Montgomery County Jail in Lima, Ohio, in September 1933 for his known robberies.

Police found documents on his person that seemed to outline an escape from the Indiana State Prison, but Dillinger denied knowing anything about the plans and the state police captain refused to acknowledge their veracity. A few days after Dillinger's arrest, ten of his convict friends escaped that very prison using their accomplice's carefully organized schemes. They shot two guards, killing one of them on the way out with smuggled weapons.

The very next month, six of the escaped convicts came for Dillinger, who had been transferred to a much smaller jail a few days earlier. Disguised as officers from the Indiana State Prison, they told the sheriff they had come to return Dillinger to Indiana for violating his parole, but they were missing the final touch on their dastardly plan: credentials. When the sheriff asked to see identification, one of

Dillinger's men pulled a gun on him and beat him, stealing the keys that would free their beloved gang leader. To make sure they weren't followed, they locked the sheriff's wife and the deputy in a cell, leaving the sheriff to perish from his wounds.

When reporters went to Dillinger's father for a comment on the escape, he said that if his son had received a lighter sentence when he was arrested for the first robbery, he might not have strayed so far down the path of darkness. The senior Dillinger never attempted to get involved with his son's crimes nor did he try to stop him; he simply went about his life, taking care of the farm and silently pitying his son.

Neither Dillinger nor his accompanying fugitives had violated federal law, yet the FBI was pulled in to identify and find the criminals behind the escape. When they were identified, Dillinger's faceless gang suddenly had names: Harry "Pete" Pierpont, Russell Lee "Boobie" Clark, John "Red" Hamilton, and Charles "Fat Charley" Makley were officially wanted men.

In December 1933, the Chicago Police Department formed the Dillinger Squad, a special unit whose main goal was to track down and kill John Dillinger. Just two weeks after this group was formed, the Illinois Crime Commission included the notorious bank robber in a list of the state's most wanted criminals, alongside his other cronies, together known as the Dillinger Gang.

With the FBI hot on their trail, the Dillinger Gang raced across Indiana, where the young gangster and his band of criminals plundered banks and police arsenals in Auburn and Peru. Their collection of machine guns, rifles, revolvers, and even bullet-proof vests grew as they tore through the countryside. They were interested only in robbing banks; innocent bystanders could keep the money in their wallets or purses. Dillinger wanted to intimidate on a national scale, which is partly why the public admired him so much. One of the men shot a Chicago detective dead that December, and Dillinger himself killed a police officer after a robbery at the First National Bank of East Chicago.

The group decided to split and head west, lie low for a while, and meet up in Tucson, Arizona, for a winter holiday. But when they arrived in January 1934, they were taken into custody after an ambush by police officers. Dillinger and his gang were brought to Crown Point, Indiana, to await trial for murder in a supposedly escape-proof jail. Dillinger went kicking and screaming, vowing that another jail wouldn't hold him for long.

Holding true to his word, the young bank robber made plans to break loose with a wooden gun smuggled in by one of the jail officers through Dillinger's attorney. On March 3, 1934, Dillinger threatened a guard passing by his cell, waving the faux gun with aggressive intent. He not only forced the guard to open his cell door but also locked him inside, bragging about the wooden toy as he made his escape. He then stole two real machine guns, which made it much easier to exit the prison alongside another inmate, Herbert Youngblood, who was on trial for murder. Together, they stole the sheriff's car and fled through Illinois toward St. Paul, Minnesota.

While the other members of the original Dillinger Gang were locked up for their crimes, Homer Van Meter was one of the few who hadn't been caught in the most recent sweep of arrests. He enlisted the help of the infamous George "Baby Face" Nelson, who would join the gang only if Dillinger could take orders. Agreeing grudgingly to let Nelson lead the gang, Van Meter anxiously awaited Dillinger's escape from Crown Point. Meeting up in St. Paul for the first time on March 5, 1934, Nelson and Dillinger instantly joined forces, creating a much stronger, second wave of the Dillinger Gang.

By stealing the sheriff's car and crossing state lines from Indiana into Illinois, Dillinger had finally violated a federal law. This gave the FBI an excellent excuse to get fully involved in the hunt for John Dillinger. Director J. Edgar Hoover gave the case to special agent Samuel A. Cowley, who set up camp in Chicago with special agent Melvin Purvis. Allying with East Chicago cops, the small task force tracked down every tip they received in hopes of nabbing Dillinger, the man on the run.

In the twisted and mangled FBI chase from Chicago to St. Paul to Warsaw and on through Michigan and Wisconsin, Dillinger got his girlfriend, Evelyn "Billie" Frechette, involved in his criminal schemes. Together, they visited Dillinger's family farm in Mooresville on April 7, where he spoke with his father about going away for a long while. Then they left for Chicago, and the very next day, Billie was arrested at a diner and eventually convicted of harboring a fugitive; she was slapped with a two-year prison sentence.

Dillinger was losing friends and gang members to police consistently at this point, and he was running out of places to hide.

On June 22, 1934, John Dillinger was named Public Enemy Number One. It was the bank robber's birthday. The next day, a $10,000 reward was placed on Dillinger's head, $5,000 on Nelson's, and a shoot-to-kill order on both of them.

Agent Cowley received a tip just a month later from a woman who called herself Anna Sage. She was born Ana Cumpanas, an immigrant from Romania, and wanted protection from deportation plus the $10,000 reward Hoover had placed on Dillinger's head in exchange for information. Though cautious, Cowley agreed to meet with her and pay her only if the tip led to Dillinger's arrest. She complied.

Sage told Cowley and Purvis that she, her friend Polly Hamilton, and none other than the notorious gangster himself would be at a theater in Chicago to see a film the following evening. Dillinger was hiding out with them, she explained, but went by an alias to disguise himself. She would call the agents to confirm which venue they would attend as soon as she knew and would wear an orange dress to be easier to find.

Dillinger was playing with the law at this point, possibly testing the limits of his assumed invincibility. He once walked into a Chicago police station, inquiring about a nonexistent inmate, and even attended a Chicago Cubs game at the world-famous Wrigley Field. But that summer, Dillinger stepped over the line.

On July 22, around 8:30 p.m., Sage, Hamilton, and Dillinger waltzed into the Biograph Theater to see Clark Gable in *Manhattan Melodrama*, the latest film about American gangsters. The police were alerted and quickly surrounded the venue while the trio was inside, but officers were instructed not to breach the theater to spare innocent moviegoers from any crossfire.

When Dillinger walked out of the theater around 10 p.m., a lady on each arm, he turned left, where agent Purvis was standing with a cigar in hand. Dillinger took no note of the man. Anna Sage's orange dress looked crimson in the moonlight, earning her the nickname "Lady in Red" in retellings of the event.

Purvis was meant to light the cigar as a signal to his agents, but he was so nervous that he failed to spark the match. The surrounding officers all caught the cue anyway, just as Sage slowed to avoid getting shot. Hamilton noticed the move and tried to warn Dillinger, but bullets were already ripping through the air. Dillinger quickly flipped his pistol out of his right pants pocket, darting down an alley away from the gunfire.

It was over before it even began. Only five shots were fired, but three of them hit Dillinger. Down he went, face first, onto the cobbled street. With a shot through the left side, one grazing his face, and the other into his back, John Dillinger was pronounced dead at 10:51 p.m. at the nearby Alexian Brothers Hospital.

No one was sure who shot Dillinger first, but the three officers who fired—Charles B. Winstead, Clarence O. Hurt, and Herman E. Hollis—were commended by Hoover for their courage and resolution under pressure. Dillinger's body was put on public display, and more than fifteen thousand visitors came to get a last look at the infamous gangster.

In the end, twenty-seven people were convicted of concealing or aiding John Dillinger in his multitude of crimes over the years. Eleven members of the Dillinger Gang were killed while on the run, and twenty-three others ended up in federal prison. Dillinger racked up more than $300,000 throughout his bank-robbing career, defining him as one of the most notorious criminals of his time.

John Dillinger was buried in Crown Hill Cemetery in Indianapolis, Indiana, some 180 miles south of Chicago, inevitably putting an end to the gangster era.

CHAPTER FIVE

William Heirens

Questionable Conviction of the Lipstick Killer

ONE OF THE MOST HEINOUS CRIMES EVER COMMITTED IN Chicago put a teenager behind bars for the rest of his life, never to see the outside world again. He was Chicago's longest-serving prisoner, having spent more than sixty-five years behind bars before passing away from diabetic issues in his prison cell. But he may have been wrongfully accused; he maintained his innocence throughout his sentence and claimed that he had been coerced into confessing by Chicago police.

In his youth, William Heirens was handsome and alluring, but by the end of his trial, he was disgusting to the public eye. He was nicknamed the Lipstick Killer for a plea scrawled in lipstick on the wall above a body savagely stabbed to death. The unnerving note read, "For heavens [sic] Sake catch me Before I kill more I cannot control myself." This was the second of three murders that were connected to him.

Heirens hailed from Lincolnwood, a suburb north of the city, and had a fairly normal upbringing. But, as everyone knows, normal is relative, and Heirens may have had trouble as a child dealing with his parents' failed marriage. They fought constantly, so to relieve tension in his early years, Heirens took up shoplifting and petty thievery. Whether it was cash-based or the collection of expensive clothes, radios, and weapons he built up over time, Heirens was constantly finding illegal outlets to deal with his stress.

When he was thirteen years old, Heirens was arrested for possessing a loaded gun, and when police searched his home, they found all of his stolen treasures. The sheer size of the cache was astounding, and young Heirens admitted to acquiring it all through eleven burglaries. He was sent away to Gibault School for Wayward Boys but was soon expelled and arrested for larceny.

Heirens was sentenced to three years at St. Bede Academy in Peru, Illinois, where he studied under Benedictine monks. Academic excellence was in his blood, and he transformed into a bright student skilled in mathematics and science. Having done so well on his test scores that he bypassed high school, Heirens enrolled in the University of Chicago for the 1945 fall term when he was sixteen years old. He did part-time work to meet tuition costs every year, but he also burgled at night to help cover the fees. He spent the whole year learning new things, dating girls, and making money, albeit illegally, but his good fortune was about to come to an end.

The summer before Heirens began classes at the University of Chicago, a murder went largely unnoticed in the

Chicago papers. On June 6, 1945, poor forty-three-year-old Josephine Ross was found dead in her apartment on Kenmore Avenue, just north of Wrigley Field, with a slit throat and stab wounds. Her head was wrapped in a skirt, and she had been stripped down to nothing and washed, with tape covering each of her wounds. The *Chicago Tribune* published only a small editorial about the death on page ten of the next day's paper.

Police were stumped. The apartment had been ransacked, as if robbed, but nothing was missing. There was no evidence found at the scene, save a few hairs clutched in the victim's hand. At this time, there was no way to test DNA, so the only clue they had was that the murderer was dark-haired and probably a surprised burglar. But then it happened again.

The next victim fell prey to the killer just six months later, on December 10, 1945. Thirty-two-year-old Frances Brown was found slumped over a bathtub in her apartment on Pine Grove Avenue near the north end of Lincoln Park. She had been shot and stabbed, a butcher knife still protruding from her neck. Brown was also naked, with towels wrapped around her head, and this time, police found the bone-chilling cry for help written in lipstick on the wall above her. Witnesses claimed that a nervous man, approximately 140 pounds, was seen stumbling off the premises around 4 a.m.

This time, Chicago police found a bloody fingerprint left on the doorknob, but without the technology to verify even something so distinct, it was impossible to track down the murderer. The only way they could have tested the fingerprints was if they had a suspect to compare the two.

They currently had only witness sightings and a hunch that the crimes were committed by a woman. The media wildly speculated that the murderer was a woman because of the lipstick writing on the wall and the fact that women were fond of the phrase "for heaven's sake" at the time.

So far, the media had glazed over these murders, filing them far below other stories rather than making them front-page news. The murder of an adult wasn't going to catch the eye of the public; adult deaths were more frequent and less devastating. It wasn't until the Lipstick Killer's final victim was found that Chicago was overtaken by a sense of absolute and unmitigated horror.

Six-year-old Suzanne Degnan went missing from her first-floor bedroom on January 7, 1946. Degnan lived in the Edgewater neighborhood, not very far from the previous two murders. A ransom note had been left at the scene that read, "Get $20,000 Reddy & wAITe foR WoRd. do NoT NoTify FBI oR Police. Bills IN 5's & 10's. BuRN This FoR heR SAfTY."

During the investigation, someone repeatedly called the Degnans' home but always hung up before the conversation could move forward. Chicago police were eventually notified by an anonymous caller that they should check the storm drain sewers nearby. The hint led to a horrific discovery: the six-year-old child's severed head in a sewer just a block away from her home. Other pieces of her body were discovered in various places along the sewer, in drains and a catch basin. Her blood was found pooling in the drains of a nearby apartment building's laundry facilities, indicating she had been dismembered there. Her decaying arms were found a month later in a separate location.

One of the most horrific murders to ever happen in Chicago silenced the city. Everyone waited in fear as police worked to find the killer, moving about unsuspected in the streets.

A few days after Suzanne Degnan was found, a note arrived at Chicago mayor Edward Kelly's office: "This is to tell you how sorry I am to not get ole [sic] Degnan instead of his girl. Roosevelt and the OPA made their own laws. Why shouldn't I and a lot more?"

The Degnans were part of the meatpacking industry, and nationwide meatpacking riots were happening at the time against the Office of Price Administration (OPA). Suzanne's father, James Degnan, was a senior executive with a wartime meat regulation board, meaning he was working alongside the OPA in the aftermath of World War II. Another OPA executive had received death threats against his family a few weeks earlier, and a man involved in black market meat-packing had recently been decapitated. Evidence suggested that the incisions made on little Suzanne were too exact to be just anyone; the killer must have had experience working with sharp tools to be so precise. With their hands finally on a semblance of a lead, police ran with this new information, questioning nearly every meat-packer in the city.

But another month went by and they still had no direct evidence. In a time before Miranda rights were required and people often took, in good faith, the word of those who looked like them, people in power could have told the public anything and they would have believed it. Their reputations were on the line, and Chicago police were so determined to secure a suspect that they tried to pressure the janitor of the apartment building where the Degnans lived into a confession.

They brought sixty-five-year-old Hector Verburgh in for questioning and beat him so severely that he spent ten days in the hospital. Chicago police caused him enough pain that he later claimed he would have confessed to anything had they continued. They also told the media confidently that Verburgh was their guy, even though they found out later that he was a Belgian immigrant who didn't speak enough English to have written the ominous ransom note.

By April of that year, more than three hundred suspects had been questioned, but Chicago police still hadn't pinned the deed on anyone viable. They grew increasingly desperate until they found their scapegoat.

On June 26, 1946, William Heirens made plans for a date, but he needed cash to take this girl out. He took a $1,000 note to the bank, but it was closed, so he decided to quickly rob a nearby apartment instead. Almost immediately, Chicago police responded to a call about the break-in and caught him red-handed. Apparently, Heirens pulled a gun on the cops and ran, but an off-duty officer who was returning home from the beach realized what was happening. Wearing only his swimsuit, he cast three flowerpots, one at a time, onto Heirens's head, and the suspect collapsed under the impact. Heirens was arrested and taken to a hospital.

Things quickly spiraled out of control while he was recovering. Under sedation drugs, Heirens felt his fingerprints being pressed but couldn't fight off whoever was doing it. He could hear them discussing him in connection with the Degnan case. Without a warrant, police searched his college dorm room and found stolen medical equipment and a scrapbook of Nazi officials, which Heirens had taken from a war veteran. With the end of World War II so close in the nation's memory, something like this would have terrified the public.

Somehow, all of this was enough evidence to bring Heirens in for questioning regarding the Degnan case. Heirens later claimed that for the next three days, he was tortured, starved, and beaten by Chicago police. They were adamant that he was the killer; he obviously had a criminal history, but more important, their other leads had fizzled out. After a week of mistreatment, including giving him a spinal tap without anesthesia for unknown reasons, the police slipped Heirens sodium pentothal, commonly known as the truth drug, without his consent or an official warrant. Only then did Heirens confess, claiming that he often transformed into an alternate personality called George and that his alter ego must have been the one who committed the murders.

Police pressed for George's last name, wondering if Heirens was just confused. They barely heard Heirens mumble "murmer," but police relayed that as a last name, Murman, to the press, who easily fashioned it into "Murder Man." In the public's opinion, Williams Heirens had just confessed to the murders of all three victims.

Using sodium pentothal is now recognized as an unreliable method of extracting true information; in fact scientists believe that it may cause people to make false statements. Heirens endured an immense amount of pain and stress during his interrogation and would have said anything to stop the torturous questioning. He was also given a polygraph test, but the results were inconclusive.

Following his forced confession, Heirens was indicted for assault with intent to kill, robbery, twenty-three counts of burglary, and the murders of Josephine Ross, Frances Brown, and Suzanne Degnan, all of which police claimed were linked, even though their murderers used drastically different MOs. Serial killers typically repeat the same behavior over and over, but this victim trio was a jumbled mess. The two handwritten notes were scripted differently and the methods of killing were drastically disconnected. The only true link between the three cases was that they all remained unsolved and badly needed closure.

When they compared Heirens's fingerprint to both the bloody fingerprint found on the doorknob in Brown's apartment and the fingerprint on the ransom note, just nine points of the print matched. While that's technically considered a match, fingerprints were not an exact science, and almost 65 percent of the world's population could have been linked to that print. The FBI handbook now requires twelve points of comparison to confirm identification.

At the end of a winding road of intense investigation and a subsequent murder trial, Heirens was found guilty for the murders of Ross, Brown, and Degnan. He signed a plea agreement, avoiding the death sentence thanks to the work of his lawyer, and later stated, "I confessed to save my life."

A murder without justice is the most terrifying prospect of the human race. An unsolved case means that we are all in danger; no one is spared the horrors of hell when someone can kill and get away with it. And every time one of these murders remains cold for eternity, it gives one more sick mind another reason to carry out their sinister fantasies.

While Heirens served the time for these three murders, whether or not he actually committed those crimes remains a mystery to this day. Supposing he took the fall for a murderer still on the loose turns those three deaths cold as ice and leaves a chilling imprint on the city of Chicago.

CHAPTER SIX

John Wayne Gacy

The Clown Killer's Reign of Terror

CLOWN SCARES HAVE TYPICALLY BEEN FRUITLESS CHASES, based on horrifying first impressions rather than actual danger. Very rarely do clowns actually live up to the bad reputations they're given. But there was one clown lurking in Chicago's history that deserved the fear of children, forever changing the way the face-painted jesters were seen in the public's eye. He was a danger no one saw coming, and he claimed more innocent lives than anyone could have imagined.

Over the course of his short lifetime, John Wayne Gacy was accused of brutally murdering and raping twenty-seven young boys, but there is evidence to suggest he harmed many more.

Gacy's life story is murky. By some accounts, he had a comfortable, middle-class upbringing. Behind the scenes, however, it's noted that his father was an alcoholic and often abused Gacy when he grew angry. Growing up in Chicago in the 1940s, Gacy experienced a variety of health issues as a child, which would have taken a toll on any life. And Gacy was gay, or at least struggled with his sexuality from the time he was a young boy, which would have impacted his upbringing and social life during the '50s and '60s.

Despite his same-sex preference, Gacy married Marlynn Myers in 1964. Together, they moved to Waterloo, Iowa, where Gacy settled into a job at one of his father-in-law's Kentucky Fried Chicken restaurants. Things seemed perfect from the outside, but Gacy began double-crossing his wife, spending the night with young men and making it back home in the early hours of the morning. He even missed the birth of his newborn son for a one-night stand.

During this period of his life, Gacy got involved in the Waterloo Jaycees, a group of men who hosted fundraising projects in the community. But there was also a secret side to this organization, whose members often indulged in wife-swapping, prostitution, pornography, and drugs. Gacy was regularly cheating on his wife at this point. He was named vice president of the Jaycees in 1967, and he insisted that everyone there call him the Colonel.

Many of the teenagers who worked with Gacy at KFC trusted him because he offered them alcohol. Gacy opened a club-friendly space in his basement, where his underage employees could drink and gamble without consequence. Gacy was first convicted of sexually assaulting one of his young male employees in the summer of 1967. He had promised to show a fifteen-year-old named Donald Voorhees pornography, but instead got him drunk and forced him to give Gacy oral sex. Gacy later told the young boy that he was simply testing his morals. Then he claimed he had ties to the Mafia, gave Voorhees some money, and told him to shut his mouth. Voorhees did nothing for a whole year, but, when another boy came forward to confess that Gacy had assaulted him, Voorhees also broke down and explained the incident to his father. When the public heard about the incidents, they were enraged and determined to get Gacy behind bars. But it wasn't necessarily the assault that put Gacy in prison; he was indicted on oral sodomy charges instead.

Two doctors performed an examination of Gacy over a period of seventeen days while he was being held for trial; they concluded that he had an antisocial personality disorder, an umbrella diagnosis that includes psychopathy and sociopathy. This meant he was mentally fit and able to stand trial. Marlynn divorced him immediately and on December 3, 1968, Gacy was sentenced to ten years in the Anamosa State Penitentiary for sodomy.

While in prison, Gacy received word of his father's passing in 1969 and requested leave for the funeral in Chicago, which he was ultimately denied. Gacy was convinced that his father died because of what he had done to end up in prison. He served only eighteen months before he was released on good behavior, and immediately following his release, he went back to Chicago and moved in with his mourning mother.

Together, they purchased a house at 8213 West Summerdale Avenue in Norwood Park, Chicago, but his mother didn't stay with him for long. In order to uphold his reputation in the community, Gacy decided to remarry, this time an unsuspecting woman named Carole Hoff. His mother moved out a few nights before their July 1, 1972, wedding.

When Gacy started his own contracting company in 1974, the move put him at the height of respectability in the community. His main hires were always teenage boys, as he claimed that they were more reliable than adult men to get the job done.

His wife and stepdaughters were traveling when Gacy passed the Chicago Greyhound bus station in January 1972 and caught sight of a young boy who had just arrived to the city. Promising to return him in the morning in time for his bus to Omaha, Gacy drove the boy to his home in Norwood Park and gave him a place to stay. Gacy and the boy had mutual sex, according to most accounts, but the night turned sinister when Gacy grabbed a knife and stabbed him to death. He hid the body in the crawl space, which would later attract comments from neighbors about the horrid smell.

Gacy's tale is a little different, though. He claimed later that when he awoke in the morning, he saw the teen standing in the doorway with a kitchen knife in hand, so he acted quickly. The two engaged in a violent struggle; Gacy got the upper hand and stabbed the child repeatedly in the chest before apparently experiencing a massive orgasm. He later stated in court, "That's when I realized that death was the ultimate thrill."

In 1975, Gacy joined a group of clowns called the Jolly Jokers who would regularly perform at fundraisers and parades, and who even entertained sick children at local hospitals around Chicago. Thus, the infamous Pogo the Clown was born, with Gacy dressing up in full costume and applying his own sinister makeup for Democratic conventions, charity events, and neighborhood parties. Some of the professional clowns he worked alongside noted the sharply up-turned edges to his smile, something they would typically round out to avoid scaring young kids. There is no evidence that Gacy ever murdered while donning his clown costumes, but the idea that a murderer existed behind the makeup is enough to chill the cheerful.

By the mid-1970s, homosexuality was much more widely acknowledged than it had been just a few decades before, though still not as accepted as it is today. Gacy worked up the courage to tell Carole that he preferred young men to women after they had sex on Mother's Day in 1975. She already knew this, however, as she had found male pornography hidden in places around the house. He told her he would never have sex with her again and subsequently stopped hiding the teenage boys he brought home at night to assault in the basement. Gacy and Carole divorced by mutual consent the next year and Gacy began what he called his "cruising years."

Finally alone in his home, Gacy could undertake the real breadth of his crimes. Oftentimes, his victims were his employees. Gacy would lure young men to his basement or even move them into his house if they needed a place to stay, offering them alcohol and marijuana. Gacy made it a habit to convince each young man to don handcuffs before he performed unspeakable acts of sexual abuse, torture, and eventual murder on their helpless bodies.

It was only after the disappearance of one particular teenager, Robert Piest, that police started to suspect Gacy. Piest was working at a Des Plaines pharmacy in December 1978 when Gacy overheard him talking about his salary.

Gacy offhandedly mentioned that he hired for double the pay the fifteen-year-old was making, and Piest excitedly took him up on the offer. When his mother drove by to pick him up that night, Piest promised her he would be right back; he wanted to talk with this employer about a great job opportunity. After fifteen minutes, Piest's mother started to get worried, so she went to look for her son. But she would never see him again.

This was sloppy work for Gacy. After six years of getting away with murder, he had grown lazy, possibly even believing he would never get caught. Police took note of Piest's disappearance after his mother filed a missing person's report. The case was strange; Piest was not a runaway, and his character was unblemished in the community. When police inquired about the incident at the pharmacy, employees directed them to John Wayne Gacy, the last known person to see Piest alive.

Chicago police sent a squad to Gacy's house the following night, but when he answered the door, he was abrupt and rude to them. He almost shut the door on them but promised to come down to the station later that night. A very brash Gacy showed up to the Des Plaines police station at 3:30 a.m., smeared from head to toe in wet mud. He claimed he had just been in a car accident.

That night, police ran a background check on Gacy and noticed he had been convicted for sodomy on a fifteen-year-old, a detail that isolated him as a suspect in the several unsolved disappearances of young boys over the last six years. Gacy was immediately detained at the station while police went to search his home.

Evidence was found throughout his home connecting him to multiple murders, starting with a trapdoor that led to the crawl space. Jewelry that didn't belong to Gacy was discovered, including a class ring with the initials of a boy who had been missing for years. Police also found sex toys, handcuffs, gay and child pornography, and clothing that was far too small to fit the large Gacy. One of the officers claimed to have smelled death when he entered the bathroom, and a full-blown investigation and excavation of Gacy's property ensued. They later found several corpses rotting in the vents.

Once he was arrested for his crimes, Gacy could no longer hold back claiming the credit. In 1978, Gacy confessed to the murders of over two dozen adolescent boys and young men, claiming to have stashed them away in the crawl space, all within the past six years. His remaining victims were found near the Des Plaines River or buried under the turf in his backyard.

Gacy awaited trial for two long years but then was swiftly convicted of his heinous crimes before a jury and sentenced to the death penalty in March 1980. Gacy never once showed an ounce of remorse for what he did.

There is a good amount of evidence to suggest that Gacy had accomplices, but none was charged alongside him. While many testified in court that they knew where Gacy kept the bodies, and one victim even claimed that there was another person who assisted Gacy in his attempted murder, these persons didn't have enough evidence against them for a conviction.

During his time at the Menard Correctional Center in Chester, Illinois, Gacy started creating art as a form of self-consolation, but his paintings were disturbing. They often depicted Gacy in his full clown costume as his alter ego, Pogo the Clown. This collection was on display in a Chicago gallery for several years and many of the pieces sold for thousands of dollars. Other paintings by Gacy were burned at a public gathering in 1994 that more than three thousand people attended, including some of the parents of the victims.

Gacy spent fourteen years on death row before he was killed by lethal injection on May 10, 1994. He believed, as he told his lawyer, that the state's decision to give him the death penalty would not compensate for the horrifying crimes he had committed, as they were killing him the same way he ended his victims. The last words John Wayne Gacy ever spoke were "Kiss my ass."

His final meal of choice? A bucket of Kentucky Fried Chicken.

Gacy's infernal legacy burned unmistakable scars into the minds of parents, victims who were lucky enough to escape, and children, who, if not before, were now absolutely terrified of killer clowns. Gacy changed the way society saw clowns forever—once a happy staple of American summers, now turned sinister in the wake of a serial murderer.

CHAPTER SEVEN

Homey D. Clown

How an Urban Legend Sparked Real Fear

FEAR MANIFESTS ITSELF IN UNUSUAL FORMS. SOME PEOPLE are afraid of itsy-bitsy spiders, creepy crawling up the walls of their infested apartment. Others dread tight spaces or heights that could end them if they fell. For many, it's the darkness itself, subtle in its falling, drastic in its entirety, ready to consume them in a blanket of unspoken evils that exist only come nightfall. Fear is usually irrational, a dramatized version of what could go wrong inside our own minds.

But for children in the early 1990s, fear took the form of Homey D. Clown.

Homey D. Clown came from the mind of Keenen Ivory Wayans and was intended to be a silly jester on *In Living Color*, a popular sketch comedy TV series that ran on the Fox network from April 15, 1990, to May 19, 1994. Wayans wrote, directed, and starred in this short-lived program, but it was his brother, Damon Wayans, who was cast as the hilarious ex-convict serving his parole as a party clown with a sarcastic attitude and an unforgettable catchphrase: "Homey don't play that!"

Homey D. Clown was iconic in his time, known to many children as the pinnacle of comedy. He would stare blankly at any kid on the show who asked him a stupid question, even going so far as to sock them on the head with a bag full of pennies and mutter, "I don't think so."

While the show's intent was innocent enough, the character spawned years of horror surrounding a menacing stranger who dressed up in Homey D. Clown garb and terrorized the children of Chicago. Police were never able to apprehend the man connected to the sightings, and these incidents were eventually written off as an urban legend. But to the kids who saw him, it was real enough.

In the fall of 1991, the rumors started in the weeks leading up to Halloween, threatening the safety of Chicago's youth. Claims that some sordid character was disguising himself as the much-loved television persona and luring children to a white van with promises of candy and money sprouted up all over the city. An article published in the *Chicago Tribune* on October 11, 1991, described an African American man standing 5-foot-11 and weighing 175 pounds, a very specific description for someone who eternally evaded the police. The reported color of the van varied from red to white, brown, or blue, but always with the words "Ha-Ha" scripted on its side door. Other reports cited the evil Homey driving a black pickup truck or a dark-colored Oldsmobile, which made the police skeptical of its existence at all. These variations could have meant that there were several Homey D. Clown impersonators roaming the streets.

Whether by intentional collusion or not, these jesters spread panic throughout Chicago schools and the homes of local residents.

It was a scary time for clowns all over the city. Police conducted random searches, stopping anyone dressed in what might have been their usual work clothes to investigate clowns and find the culprit. That meant discrimination, especially against black and Latino clown workers, who are statistically pulled over more frequently as is, but now also faced harassment from people who saw them in costume.

Homey D. Clown sightings were noted at four schools in Gary, Indiana, and several more across the Chicago area, including Jefferson Elementary School, St. Ann Catholic School in Lansing, Washington Irving Elementary School, LeMoyne School, and Reavis Elementary Math and Science Specialty School. An official letter issued to parents of the Oak Park Elementary School District warned that it was a rumor that may have gotten out of hand, but school officials were taking every necessary precaution just in case.

Children hurried home quicker than ever and doors were hastily closed behind them. Even parents started asking school boards if there had been any sightings of Homey D. Clown nearby. In the wake of Clown Killer John Wayne Gacy's arrest a decade previous, it was no wonder that a clown scare was alive and well just two years before his death.

But no more stories were published by the newspapers and Chicago police never made any arrests in connection to the rumors. Speculation eventually spread throughout schools that Homey D. Clown was killed off by a notorious Chicago gang or otherwise moved out of town to avoid arrest. Chicago police waved it all off as an urban legend, refusing to give weight to these stories. During their vigilance, no violent crimes were committed by a clown.

Clown sightings are not unique to Chicago. In the decades after the Homey D. Clown scare, there have been more than a few sinister clown scares and sightings by both children and adults. While killings by people dressed as clowns are rare, the number of valid creepy sightings of clowns terrorizing or chasing community members all across America increased drastically between 1991 and now. But no clown since Gacy has been convicted of murder, rape, or child abduction, at least not according to police reports.

To this day, there is no way to track down who actually saw a person dressed like Homey D. Clown. It was always someone's friend's cousin who had heard of Homey terrorizing the schoolyard, or some other distant relation. But never a handed-down true sighting from one person to the next.

A common thread in most clown sightings is an element of fear. But they also typically lack any actual violence or action. People are instantly frightened by the sight of clowns, even if they aren't doing anything to seem threatening. In its entirety, that can be blamed on the media. Homey D. Clown was a sarcastic ex-convict with a bad temper. Stephen King's Pennywise literally ate children. And all of this was popular culture of the time, and it may have heightened the fear in Chicago's youths.

Those kids weren't seeing a singular person dressed as Homey D. Clown, wandering the streets of Chicago, ready to kidnap youngsters and terrorize them to death. They pinned that title on any clown they saw, and because Homey

D. Clown was such a popular character during that time, every sighting was associated with him.

Fear can ignite and fan falsehoods into flame so quickly that not even the truth can extinguish it. The Homey D. Clown scare of 1991 was proof of that. All it might have taken was one clown to scare one child for the stories to spark. After a single sighting, it would have spread like wildfire, because fear, like flame, manifests in all of us.

PART II
UNCOVERING CHICAGO'S UNJUST TRAGEDIES

View of overturned SS *Eastland* in the Chicago River, with holes cut in hull, Chicago, Illinois, July 24, 1915. Rescue crew can be seen on top of the overturned ship. CHICAGO HISTORY MUSEUM, ICHI-033119; JUN FUJITA, PHOTOGRAPHER

CHAPTER EIGHT

The Treaty of Chicago

Uprooting the Potawatomi Tribe

LONG BEFORE FEUDS BETWEEN ITALIAN AND IRISH MOB-
sters tore up the city streets, the Chicagoland area was home
to the Bodéwadmi tribe, a group of Native American people
that had grown wide and strong across the Great Plains,
on the north side of the Mississippi River, and throughout
the Great Lakes region. Anglicized as Potawatomi, their
language stemmed from the Algonquin tongue, which was
spoken in a large section of eastern Canada, the Upper Pen-
insula, northeast America, and, of course, the area that later
developed into Chicago.

The removal of the Bodéwadmi people from the Chicagoland region was a slow-creeping slug with a venomous
trail. When the United States was established in 1776, white
Americans began the process of forcibly taking land from
Native American tribes and grouping them into a concen-
trated area known as Indian Territory, which is modern-day
Oklahoma. These treaties, named after the territories they
claimed, essentially required Native American people to

surrender their lands. The United States then completely owned and took control over the ceded region and physically uprooted the Native American people who lived there.

When a Native American confederation signed the Treaty of Greenville in 1795, the agreement reached into a six-mile stretch of land at the mouth of the Chicago River. The United States was closing in and Native tribes had nowhere to go. White people quite literally displaced and regrouped indigenous people into isolated areas, steadily colonizing North America and stripping its culture away one treaty at a time.

Just two decades later, the 1816 Treaty of St. Louis allowed the United States to creep even closer to the Bodéwadmi region, seizing a large chunk of the north side of Illinois, southeast of the Mississippi River. Illinois officially became the twenty-second state on December 2, 1818, and was incorporated into Michigan Territory, which covered a wide stretch of Michigan south of the Grand River and all of Wisconsin, Minnesota, and Iowa, from 1818 to 1833. From 1833 to 1836, the area expanded to include parts of North and South Dakota to the east of the Missouri River. A few solitary reservations were established in order to quarantine Native American tribes to a small section of land that would remain under their own control. Standing Rock Indian Reservation and the Cheyenne River Reservation still stand today in the northern half of South Dakota.

The east side of Illinois and the north side of Indiana were swept into this massive region when the Treaty of Chicago was developed because they both directly touched Lake Michigan. The first Treaty of Chicago was signed on August

29, 1821, and put into effect on March 25, 1822, ceding all lands in the Michigan Territory to the United States.

Michigan territorial governor Lewis Cass, alongside jurist Solomon Sibley, met with members of the Council of Three Fires to discuss the impending treaty on August 29. The Bodéwadmi people were part of the Council of Three Fires, a longstanding alliance that also included the Odaawaa (anglicized as Ottawa) and the Ojibwe (anglicized as Chippewa).

Bodéwadmi Chief Metea argued against selling the territories to white Americans who planned to colonize the wild lands. He initially followed the custom of all Native American people, which was to acknowledge what the other party had said and then deliberate over the treaty before signing. When the group reconvened, Chief Metea made a strong argument in defense of his homeland and future generations of Native people. He spoke passionately, with melancholic anger and valid concern. But the truth was that the Council of Three Fires had no choice—if its members didn't cede their lands, the United States would wage war with them. After centuries of trying and failing to protect their lands, Native American people preferred a peaceful settlement to the violence they had already endured, even if it meant vicious colonization. They were resigned to sell their homes instead of being pilfered. Chief Metea articulated the difficulty of this decision:

We meet you here to-day, because we had promised it, to tell you our minds, and what we have agreed upon among ourselves. You will listen to us with a good mind, and believe what we say. You know that we first came to this country, a long time ago, and when we sat ourselves down upon it, we met with a great many hardships and difficulties. Our country was then very large; but it has dwindled away to a small spot, and you wish to purchase that! This has caused us to reflect much upon what you have told us; and we have, therefore, brought all the chiefs and warriors, and the young men and women and children of our tribe, that one part may not do what others object to, and that all may be witnesses of what is going forward. You know your children. Since you first came among them, they have listened to your words with an attentive ear, and have always hearkened to your counsels. Whenever you have had a proposal to make to us, whenever you have had a favor to ask of us, we have always lent a favorable ear, and our invariable answer has been "yes." This you know! A long time has passed since we first came upon our lands, and our old people have all sunk into their graves. They had sense. We are all young and foolish, and do not wish to do anything that they would not approve, were they living. We are fearful we shall offend their spirits, if we sell our lands; and we are fearful we shall offend you, if we do not sell them. This has caused us great perplexity of thought, because we have counselled among ourselves, and do not know how we can part with the land. Our country was given to us by the Great Spirit, who gave it to us to hunt upon, to make our cornfields upon, to live upon, and to make down our beds upon when we die. And he would never forgive us, should we bargain it away. When you first spoke to us for lands at St. Mary's, we said we had a little, and agreed to sell you a piece of it; but we told you we could spare no more. Now you ask us again. You are never satisfied! We have sold you a great tract of land already; but it is not enough! We sold it to you for the benefit of your children, to farm and to live upon. We have now but little left. We shall want it all for ourselves. We know not how long we may live, and we wish to have some lands for our children to hunt upon. You are gradually taking away our hunting-grounds. Your children are driving us before them. We are growing uneasy. What lands you have, you may retain forever; but we shall sell no more. You think, perhaps, that I speak in passion; but my heart is good towards you. I speak like one of your own children. I am an Indian, a red-skin, and live by hunting and fishing, but my country is already too small; and I do not know how to bring up my children, if I give it all away. We sold you a fine tract of land at St. Mary's. We said to you then, it was enough to satisfy your children, and the last we should sell: and we thought it would be the last you would ask for. We have now told you what we had to say. It is what was determined on, in a council among ourselves; and what I have spoken, is the voice of my nation. On this account, all our people have come here to listen to me; but do not think we have a bad opinion of you. Where should we get a bad opinion of you? We speak to you with a good heart, and the feelings of a friend. You are acquainted with this piece of land—the country we live in. Shall we give it up? Take notice, it is a small piece of land, and if we give it away, what will become of us? The Great Spirit, who has provided it for our use, allows us to keep it, to bring up our young men and support our families. We should incur his anger, if we bartered it away. If we had more land, you should get more; but our land has been wasting away ever since the white people became our neighbors, and we have now hardly enough left to cover the bones of our tribe. You are in the midst of your red children. What is due to us in money, we wish, and will receive at this place; and we want nothing more. We all shake hands with you. Behold our warriors, our women, and children. Take pity on us and on our words.

Regardless of Chief Metea's pleas against the 1821 Treaty of Chicago, the Council of Three Fires signed over all of the Michigan Territory, as it was defined at the time, to the United States. By 1833, another treaty was formed under the same name, but this time, the United States wanted even more territory. The second Treaty of Chicago acknowledged that all lands west of Lake Michigan to Lake Winnebago, Wisconsin, including the region that would eventually be home to the Windy City, were now under the control of the United States. In return, the Bodéwadmi were promised cash payments, which was another deceptive method of colonization, as it forced Native people to accept the American dollar as the universal currency in their lands. Chicago was already forming as a town in 1833, and the United States wanted the region cleansed of Native tribes to make way for new developments.

Chief Metea was right: no matter how much land the white man seized, it was never enough.

When the second Treaty of Chicago went into effect in 1835, more than five hundred Native warriors gathered for the last time in the Chicago area to perform a final war dance, gracefully adorned in traditional garb and brandishing tomahawks. The Bodéwadmi were then forced from their homes and sent west, where they remained segregated on Indian reservations for generations. Chicago was incorporated as a city just two years later, in 1837.

Why the Native people gave up their lands is no mystery. From the first moment settlers from all over the world began encroaching on their territory three hundred years earlier, they resisted colonization, only for war to ensue and force them out anyway. They had no choice; it was subjugation or death.

Initial battles broke out between the English, later French settlers, and the Native tribes over the next few decades. These conflicts eventually resulted in full-scale wars, including the French and Indian War, which was the American phase of the Seven Years' War, and the Northwest Indian War, a direct result of the American Revolutionary War. When the British surrendered, they signed the Treaty of Paris in 1783, which allowed the new Americans to gain control over Ohio and Illinois country, disregarding the Native American people who already lived there.

Several more deadly conflicts ensued, one of which was the Battle of Fort Dearborn, which took place in the Chicago region during the War of 1812. Fort Dearborn staked a claim on the south bank of the Chicago River in what is the modern-day Loop area of downtown Chicago. At the time, it was recognized as a sweeping wilderness, unclaimed territory in the eyes of white Americans. But that's where they were wrong.

It was days before Captain Nathan Heald heard of the collapse of modern Michigan's Fort Mackinac on July 29, 1812, which was not far enough from Fort Dearborn to guarantee their exemption from the same fate. He immediately ordered the evacuation of the Chicago-based fort, enlisting the help of the Bodéwadmi for safe escort to Fort Wayne in exchange for ammunition, firearms, and whiskey. But instead of holding up his promise, he had all of those goods destroyed as they left Fort Dearborn, because he feared what the Native Americans would do with them. Because Heald broke his end of the deal, the Bodéwadmi ambushed fort residents as they were leaving and bloodshed ensued. The battle lasted only fifteen minutes before the Bodéwadmi took the few survivors captive and ransomed them off, one of the tribe's final victories before the United States completely overwhelmed it.

The Indian Removal Act was signed into law on May 28, 1830, by President Andrew Jackson and was heavily enforced through the presidency of Martin Van Buren, until 1841. Under this new law, the president could negotiate with southern Native American tribes, though their deal was rather sour: in exchange for white settlement in their ancestral lands, which was somehow slated as a good thing, every tribe had to relocate to federal territory in the West. Native tribes would receive small installments of money as a pathetic excuse for a gesture of peace. Once again, there was really no choice involved here. The Indian Removal Act has since been considered massive systematic genocide because it stripped Native American tribes of their culture and homeland and ensured their deaths. The most pronounced proof is the Cherokee Nation's fatal venture west, better known as the Trail of Tears, in 1838.

The American Indian Center in Albany Park, Chicago, was established in the Uptown neighborhood in 1953, making it the oldest urban sanctuary for Native American people in the country. The center's initial job was to help Native Americans get well-adjusted to city living during the Indian Relocation Act of 1956, which, again, uprooted Native people and dispersed them to major cities. This legislation ended federal recognition of several tribes, as well as discontinued funding for services like schools and hospitals on federal reservations. Chicago was on the list of places to which Native Americans were allowed to relocate; more than sixty-five thousand Native people live there today, representing approximately 175 tribes.

Chicago is a great city, but its origins remain tethered to bloodshed and forcible colonization. While residents of the metropolis should celebrate Chicago's evolution into one of the greatest cities in the world, let them never forget the reason it exists in the first place.

Chapter Nine

Lager Beer Riot

Immigrant Power against Ethnic Bias

Civil disobedience is a key democratic right, a cornerstone of major turning points in American history. Protesting, peaceful or not, has always raised mass awareness, as well as some fear, ultimately impacting the way citizens think, act, and vote. The democratic way has always been about appealing to the majority, refusing to succumb to the harmful beliefs of small extremist groups, and protecting the rights of human beings, regardless of their background, as a whole.

The first civil disturbance in the city of Chicago came in a flash on April 21, 1855. The Lager Beer Riot was a major turning point for political partisanship, mobilizing immigrant voters to make a difference in their communities, especially when under attack from unjust laws created by racist politicians. It was a moment of empowerment, heroism, and community, one that continues to affect the American voting system today.

Prior to the Lager Beer Riot, Chicago's city elections were counted as disinteresting by the average citizen. A small group of anti-immigrant and anti-Catholic "nativists"—known today as "extremists"—ran the show during election time. Mayors were given office based on their popularity within a small political party called the Know-Nothings, which was primarily interested in moral reform, public order, and privatized municipal services. It was easy to get who they wanted in office without any kind of backlash. The Know-Nothing Party officially called itself the American Party, but it earned the name "Know-Nothings" because members claimed they knew nothing of their own group when asked.

In 1855, the Know-Nothing's mayoral candidate, Levi Boone, capitalized on their xenophobic motivations, vowing to make major changes in Chicago that would force immigrants out, or at least make them uncomfortable in their own homes, even though most American citizens were once immigrants to the United States.

Boone's administration wanted immigrants to spend a minimum of twenty-one years in America before applying for citizenship and it certainly didn't want them running for office. German and Irish immigrants were targeted by American-born citizens both for their ethnicity and their religious differences and were even barred from city jobs during Boone's term.

Mayor Boone followed through on his campaign promise when he passed a "Law and Order" coalition on March 6, 1855, which was racially biased and altogether cruel to its victims. This meant hiking liquor license fees to $300— equivalent to almost $9,000 in 2020—and shortening the license terms from one year to three months. The goal was to put German- and Irish-owned pubs out of business, eventually driving them out of town.

Knowing there would be counteraction, Boone also made changes to the police force, tripling the number of officers and turning it into a menacing group of uniform-wearing, anti-immigrant oppressors who were instructed to enforce the closing of taverns and saloons on Sundays. This rule was truly enforced only in immigrant communities, primarily German and Irish neighborhoods. This upset the locals in these areas, who labored hard during their six-day work-weeks and communally rested on Sunday afternoons at local bars.

Headstrong bar owners refused to pay the outrageous license fees, let alone close up shop on their busiest day of the week. Arrests were made, and it was only a matter of time before city courts were flooded with civil disobedience cases. Roughly two hundred tavern owners were awaiting trial on charges of violating the Sunday law. Attorneys set a test case for April 21, hoping to find a standard by which to discipline the majority after resolving a single case. But what they actually did was schedule a riot.

On April 21, 1855, crowds formed outside the courthouse to protest their favorite bars no longer serving liquor or to take a stand for their fellow immigrant neighbors. Whatever the case, the throng was large enough to be considered a full-blown riot. Locals began loading up guns, preparing for a fight they knew would ensue, and Mayor Boone began to panic. He sent his police force into the crowd to disperse it, which resulted in nine initial arrests.

The German community, which was settled into the North Side at this point in time, would not stand for it. An armed group was formed in opposition to the police, their goal to rescue the unfortunate nine, but Mayor Boone was prepared for this retaliation. It was as simple as keeping the Clark Street drawbridge raised until he could gather a larger police force that would overpower the riotous group, now angrily storming the streets of Chicago. Mayor Boone alerted the National Guard of the violence that was about to occur.

The drawbridge was finally lowered when more than two hundred policemen and two cannons were stationed in front of city hall. A battle commenced, and police fired at the crowds that raged toward them. Armed protesters fired back, and the short-lived conflict resulted in dozens wounded but just one death: rioter Peter Martin shot policeman George W. Hunt in the arm before other officers shot and killed Martin. Hunt's arm was amputated after the battle. Though it was all over in a matter of minutes, murmurs of even more dead spread like a plague through the crowds, mostly due to the menacing cannons looming over the steps of city hall. No one would be held accountable for the death of the activist.

Chicago voter turnout increased in the following years, especially among immigrant voters exercising their American rights. In 1856, German and Irish voters overturned the nativists and were able to restore liquor license fees to $50 per year, just like the good old days. Mayor Boone didn't even stand for reelection, his career destroyed by his petty mistakes. Never before had Chicago seen such a high voter turnout rate, but it would only increase over time as civilians continued to disagree with the way elected officials wielded their power.

Immigrant turnout made a difference then, just as it does today. Though racists, xenophobes, and extremists will tend to disagree, every vote counts. Civil disobedience is a democratic freedom, even a responsibility to protect the basic human rights of all. That's the American way.

CHAPTER TEN

The Great Chicago Fire

The Lawless Aftermath

THE GREAT CHICAGO FIRE IS ONE OF THOSE STORIES THAT
will forever haunt the minds of Windy City natives and
their offspring. Passed down from generation to generation,
the infamous legend of Catherine O'Leary's cow and the
blazing inferno that swept the city are vivid images that,
even with all survivors of the fire now gone, still burn bright
against the skyline. The crackling of the flames and screams
of terrified souls are sounds all too familiar for a generation
that has no recollection of the actual incident. Memories are
powerful and were easily passed on to the next era of cau-
tious architects, prepared to build the city more fire-proof
and indestructible than ever before.

Everyone has heard the legend that the O'Learys' cow
kicked over a lantern and instigated one of the most horrendous episodes in Chicago history. Many dismiss this theory,
but the fire did originate near the O'Leary residence at 137
DeKoven Street on the southwest side. Whether their cow
kicked over a lantern or not, the O'Learys denied that they

had anything to do with it and the cause of the fire is still unknown today.

While the flames themselves were enough to wipe out a third of the city's wooden streets and buildings, few know that the true tragedy came after the ash had settled.

The Great Chicago Fire burned for exactly two days, from October 8 to October 10, 1871, and devastated over four miles of the city. The inferno left more than 300 people dead in its wake and roughly one hundred thousand people homeless, as well as decimated over $200 million worth of property in structural damages. That left a lot of homes totally destroyed, but many with abandoned possessions still up for the taking. It didn't take long for looting and other criminal activity to run rampant through Chicago.

Firefighters were the most essential persons in the city at the time, but even with every single station in Chicago on duty, they couldn't stop the fire from spreading. It was simply too all-encompassing, extending north and east from its origin, eventually consuming all of what is now known as the Loop, as well as Chicago's North Side, stretching far past Lincoln Park. Ironically, the O'Leary house was spared entirely, as it stood upwind from the flames.

If not for merciful rainfall on the third day, it's unclear how long and widespread the Great Chicago Fire might have been.

Soldiers were ushered into the city on October 11, just a day after the conflagration had ceased, when Chicago mayor Roswell B. Mason declared a state of martial law. In the midst of the fire, Chicago was under attack by its own citizens, so General Philip Sheridan was placed in charge of rounding up criminals and putting the lawlessness to rest. It took only a few days for the looting to slow, so martial law was lifted in the week following the destruction.

The Great Chicago Fire was bound to happen, according to historians. Many of the city's streets and buildings were made entirely of wood, leaving the whole scape flammable from the start. After the destruction of the Great Chicago Fire, the city lay in ruins, and many people probably believed that Chicago would never be the same again. They would have been right, but that didn't mean its citizens would stay helpless for long.

A *Chicago Tribune* headline following the aftermath read, "Chicago will rise from the ashes!" And rise it did. The Windy City had its own destiny, not to be derailed by one of the most infamous tragedies to affect the United States. Chicago recovered in an exceptionally quick amount of time, thanks to the combined efforts of its citizens and officials. Once the rubble was cleared away, it was almost as if the fire gave everyone a clean slate upon which to build the great Second City. The whole metropolis was up for the challenge, ready to pave the way to a future brighter even than the flames that had just devoured their homes. Everyone participated in creating a new and improved Chicago: saloon hours were limited to prevent more looting, wagon drivers were not to overcharge for their services, and even smoking was banned for a short time.

The repercussions of the fire prompted the rise of stone and brick construction, and eventually the world's first steel-structure skyscraper, toward the end of the 1800s. Chicago embodied a phoenix over the course of the next few decades, rising to the height of innovation when it hosted the 1893 world's fair just twenty-one years after the conflagration.

Today, Chicago is known across the globe as one of the greatest cities in existence. Whether that is because of its expansion, or its citizens, is up to the individual.

CHAPTER ELEVEN

The *Eastland* Disaster

Lake Michigan's Deadliest Shipwreck

WHEN UNEXPECTED HORROR STRIKES, WITH DEATH NIP-
ping at its heels, humans often react in one of two ways:
fight or flight. In a moment, fear can take a brave soul and
reduce him to nothing, evoking buried survival instincts, an
"every man for himself" ethos.

And yet, in other situations, fear can make warriors out
of ordinary people. It can bring out a seamless cooperation
to save the lives of the group, rather than just oneself. Sta-
tus, gender, nationality, political stance, and other differences
fade away until all you can see from a distance is one humanity, finally working together.

Why is it only in the worst of times that we put away
our ignorance?

A great number of shipwrecks litter the depths of Lake
Michigan, but few people are conscious of the fact that Chicago's Great Lake is home to one of the most horrific shipwrecks in history. The *Eastland* disaster took more passenger

lives than the *Lusitania* or the *Titanic*, though few seem to remember the Midwest's largest shipwreck.

On July 24, 1915, passengers stepped across the gang-plank to board the *Eastland*, which was set to sail southeast along Lake Michigan to Washington Park in Michigan City, Indiana, for an all-day outing. Western Electric was having its fifth annual employee picnic, and the entire company was invited to celebrate. Large families stood alongside eager singles, all excited about the opportunity for a day off from work at this unusually large social gathering.

One of five boats prepared to sail that day, the *Eastland* was scheduled as the first to leave, so the crew had boarded early and ushered people quickly on board at a rate of about fifty per minute. Two federal inspectors kept count, per usual, to uphold the *Eastland*'s 2,000-person maximum capacity. But the number of passengers and crew that day totaled 2,573, an oversight that some later thought was unforgivable.

It was raining that day, so many of the passengers went belowdecks to stay dry. As soon as all passengers were boarded and ready for their trip, the 265-foot-long boat started to teeter, just a little, toward its port side away from the dock.

A slight tilt like this was considered normal, or at least unexceptional, due to a slight imbalance of weight distribution across the deck as people boarded. The majority of passengers and crew assumed nothing was wrong when the boat tipped back to its starboard side, but soon it began rocking to and fro until it tilted so sharply to port that it hovered just for a moment, aching to right itself. By the time the harbormaster and the crowd that had gathered for send-off realized what was happening, there was no rectifying the situation. The boat was not coming back up.

When the gangway on the boat's port side reached the surface of the river, fresh water poured through openings, flooding the engine room and startling the crew below. Only then did they fully understand the gravity of the situation. Captain Harry Pedersen sounded the alarm to evacuate the ship, but this warning came far too late. It was only a few minutes later that the entire boat was tilted at a 45-degree angle, destined to sink.

In the midst of the chaos, everything on the boat began to shift. A refrigerator toppled over, pinning passengers beneath it, and a grand piano crushed two women to death when it slid across the deck. Water rushed into the cabins, preventing anyone below from reaching the surface ever again. Those who tried to escape up the stairs were pinned in the hallway as the floods surged in. Some passengers were among the lucky, but the horror of the scene before them quickly doused any feelings of fortune.

Just two minutes after its 45-degree tilt, and before ever leaving port, the *Eastland* tipped on its side, filled with murky water, and dragged 844 lives beneath the surface of Lake Michigan. The large vessel was only twenty feet from the dock.

Humans dotted the shadowy lake, struggling to float above the poor souls dragged down to their deaths in the whirlpool caused by the sinking ship. Infants were abandoned, purposely or not, while men, women, and children tried to save themselves, gasping for air as they fought to remain above water. The survivors were able to climb aboard the side of the *Eastland*, barely even wet, but had to watch as humanity drowned in shallow water.

The onlookers snapped out of their horror and tried to help by shoving ladders and wooden crates, anything that would float, into the river. By some accounts, a man contemplating suicide that day at the riverfront instead jumped into the water and began saving lives. But their efforts only increased the chaos. People began scrambling over one another, pushing others beneath the surface in an attempt to escape. Some of the crates knocked people out as they were hit in the water. Fear had a flavor that day; it tasted like lake water.

Helen Repa, a Western Electric nurse, was the first to take real rescue and relief action toward people who escaped the river. She had tickets to board one of the other five boats scheduled for the outing that day and was on her way to the riverfront when she heard an uproar of screams. Her trolley was halted by a policeman, who explained what had happened to the *Eastland*. Already dressed in her uniform, Repa immediately left the trolley and hopped onto the back step of a passing ambulance howling its way to the scene.

Repa got right to work. She rode with some of the injured to a nearby hospital, which filled up far too quickly. There, she instructed an employee to telephone Marshall Field's for five hundred blankets to warm the soaked survivors. The department store also offered dozens of trucks to provide additional transportation since nearly every ambulance in town was screeching toward the dock. Repa also personally called several restaurants and pleaded for hot soup and coffee to be delivered to the hospital and stopped several passing automobiles, instructing their drivers to help. No one refused. Strangers loaded up their cars with *Eastland* passengers—some injured by the destruction and others simply shaken—and swiftly transported them to a hospital or back to their homes.

Almost everyone in the vicinity of the Chicago River that day flocked to the scene, eager to help and dismayed by this shocking accident. Within the hour, almost all of the survivors were back on land and cared for, leaving only the dead to pollute the river.

Emergency personnel, rescue workers, and divers were brought in to recover the unfortunate bodies, many of them women and children who had retreated belowdecks to the portside cabins upon their arrival. There was no way they could have escaped in time. The sinking of the *Eastland* happened too quickly.

Most of what historians know about the *Eastland* disaster is owed to Repa's account. Many of her statements have survived these last hundred-plus years, still shocking and dismal to the core.

"I shall never be able to forget what I saw," Repa said. "People were struggling in the water, clustered so thickly that they literally covered the surface of the river. A few were swimming; the rest were floundering about, some clinging to a little raft that had floated free, others clutching at anything they could reach—at bits of wood, at each other, grabbing each other, pulling each other down, and screaming! The screaming was the most horrible of all."

The curious case of what would have toppled such a vessel, and even more so, why more passengers' lives were claimed by the Chicago River than the high seas when the *Titanic* and the *Lusitania* went down, is a matter of physics. Though it may seem ideal to have enough lifeboats to accommodate almost every passenger on board, this actually proved to be a serious hazard in the case of the *Eastland*. The increased number of lifeboats was new legislation, signed into law by President Woodrow Wilson just a few months prior to the *Eastland* disaster. In the wake of the horrific events of the *Titanic*, Congress passed a bill that required all vessels to accommodate every passenger in case of emergency. But the *Eastland* somersaulted so quickly that it was impossible to unleash the life rafts in time.

The *Eastland* was always historically unstable. Designed initially for local excursions, the vessel wasn't built for long trips or to carry hundreds of pounds of extra weight, even after modifications were made. In order for any boat to float and not topple, it must have the proper metacentric height, which translates to the distance between a fully upright ship and the point at which it will capsize. A boat the size of the *Eastland* would have required at least a two- to four-foot metacentric height. But, through all of the changes the *Eastland* underwent over the years, that number was reduced to just four inches. Also lacking a keel and being exceptionally top-heavy because of the excess of life rafts, the *Eastland* should never have been boarded that day.

Civil lawsuits were filed to reclaim some kind of monetary reprisal that could never truly compensate for the loss of over eight hundred lives, but they dragged on for nearly two decades with little victory. Several members of the crew, including Captain Harry Pedersen and Chief Engineer Joseph Erickson, were taken into custody, partially for their own safety from grieving but angry crowds. In the end, though Pederson had the evidence stacked against him for his negligence, no one was convicted. A civil case then unfolded, and the blame was pinned largely on Erickson for mismanaging the ballast tanks and failing to right the *Eastland* before its upset. It was easy to condemn him, as he died before the civil case ended twenty-four years later.

On July 24, 1915, the Chicago River claimed the lives of 844 people when the *Eastland* tipped on its side just twenty feet from the dock. But somehow this tragedy has evaded the minds of even diehard Chicagoans, becoming a faded memory over the decades.

The president of the *Eastland* Disaster Historical Society, Ted Wachholz, shared his thoughts on why with *Smithsonian* magazine in 2014. There wasn't a single celebrity on board. No one of fame or wealth. All of the passengers were "hardworking, salt-of-the-earth immigrant families" that wanted to enjoy a day out on the water, only to make it their final resting place.

Chapter Twelve

The Grimes Sisters

The Cold Case That Shocked the Nation

Elvis Presley was once the envy and glory of American youth, simultaneously a star, a hero, and a rebel for the fabulous 1950s. He was worshipped by adults and children alike, especially the Grimes sisters.

On Friday, December 28, 1956, Barbara and Patricia Grimes were eager to see their favorite rock'n'roll star on the silver screen for the eleventh time that season. The Brighton Theater, at 4207 Archer Avenue in Brighton Park, Chicago, was just a few blocks south of their McKinley Park home and in a busy part of town. The sisters left home around 7:30 p.m. and took the bus from Western Avenue down Archer to arrive at the theater at around 7:45 p.m.

A double feature of *Love Me Tender* was playing, featuring the starry-eyed Presley. Barbara paid $2.15 for the tickets. The girls ran into a neighbor friend, Dorothy Weinert, and her little sister in the theater, so they sat nearby and enjoyed the first showing of the film together. Dorothy and her sister left during the intermission, while the Grimes sisters went to buy a bag of popcorn for the second showing.

Barbara and Patricia had promised their mother, Lorretta, that they would be back by midnight. But the clock had struck twelve, and they weren't home. Lorretta felt panic swell like a bruise in her chest as time passed. She sent two of her other four children, Thomas and Joey, to wait for their sisters at the bus stop. Perhaps they had simply missed the last bus and would be a little late. But the boys watched several buses pass before they felt resigned to go home.

The city was no place for two teenage girls after dark. Now wracked with worry, Lorretta reported her daughters missing at 2 a.m. Barbara was fifteen and Patricia, often called Pat or Petey, was thirteen. Lorretta was divorced from her ex-husband, Joseph Grimes, and raising six children on her own. She had lost her oldest daughter two years prior; there was no telling how she would handle losing her youngest daughters as well.

When the news broke, the police and most of the country believed the girls had run off to follow Elvis on his tour of America, entirely enthralled with the Presley mania. But a more sinister explanation lurked at the back of Lorretta's mind that she just couldn't shake.

With Cook County sheriff Joseph Lohman on the case, more than one hundred officers started combing Chicago streets in search of the girls.

"Young Sisters Reported Seen in Two Places," the *Chicago Tribune* headline announced on December 31. That day was also Patricia's birthday and she had planned a party at home with eight of her best friends, complete with sodas, conversation, and plenty of cake. Lorretta still held out hope that Pat would walk through the front door just in time, but ultimately the party was cancelled at the last minute.

The *Tribune* detailed supposed sightings of the Grimes sisters, but Lorretta thought they seemed contradictory and uncharacteristic of the girls. A CTA bus driver identified the girls as having gotten off at the Western Avenue stop along his route around 11:05 p.m. on the night of their disappearance, which would have been before the end of the second showing of *Love Me Tender*. The next morning, around 9:40 a.m., an Admiral Corporation guard was passing two girls he later believed to be the Grimes sisters when he overheard their confusion about where the bus station was. He pointed it out for them, but one of them told him to shut up, which he thought was rude. Neither supposed sighting came to fruition.

Neighbors came forward with claims that they had heard screams sometime near 11:30 p.m. on the night of the sisters' disappearance. This seemed to be the first and most solid piece of evidence that police had to confirm a possible kidnapping. Still, they couldn't assume that the screams had really belonged to the Grimes sisters, so they kept searching.

Rumors reached a fever pitch after the sisters had been missing for four days. A classmate of the girls, Judy Borrow, thought she saw the sisters at Archer Street and Hamilton Avenue on Saturday. Conductor Bernard Norton thought they had boarded his Milwaukee-bound train over the weekend. The *Tribune* claimed the sisters had perhaps sought a hotel room, according to a clerk at the Unity Hotel. But even with all of these sightings, Sheriff Lohman couldn't track down a pattern that seemed logical. The leads were always running into dead ends.

Lorretta was, at this point, desperately seeking any kind of help for the sake of her daughters. She was adamant that the girls had not run away. Both Barbara and Patricia were responsible and always phoned home if they were running late or staying a few extra hours at their girlfriends' houses. Lorretta claimed they never dated, nor were they involved with anyone at the time of their disappearances. Though these things are sometimes easily hidden from parents, police found no solid evidence that even the eldest, Barbara, had a secret love interest.

Lorretta believed her girls were being held against their will somewhere. They would have come home long ago, she swore, unless they were being restrained. Sheriff Lohman took her desperation seriously, though he and many of the policemen didn't believe it themselves. Sheriff Lohman was sure the girls were still within city limits, but the countless supposed sightings came from all over Chicago and into the suburbs. All turned out to be false leads.

When Lorretta's other teenage daughter, Theresa, received an anonymous, gruesome phone call on January 2, claiming the bodies of the missing two were behind the Brighton Theater, the feverish anxiety was only heightened in the Grimes home. Of course, like all others before it, the lead turned out to be false, but it crumpled Lorretta's resolve, and she was inconsolable. It was slowly dawning on everyone that the Grimes sisters might never be found.

By January 3, the *Tribune* was grasping for words on the slowly fading story. The Grimes sisters had been missing for almost a week. There was no new information to report on and no new witnesses to interview. The search was beginning to lose steam.

Eventually, the *Tribune* picked up a lead that the girls had been seen accompanied by two teenage sailors. Oddly enough, Lorretta remembered that they had met two sailors at the Oriental Theatre in the Chicago Loop the month prior. She told police that her girls had brought the boys home for tea and they phoned each other regularly. As far as Lorretta knew, though, the last time they had spoken on the telephone was November 28, a month prior to the girls' disappearance. While the sailors were apparently only friends, not love interests, this struck a chord with Sheriff Lohman, who immediately set out to find the sailors.

He picked up the two teenage sailors, named Larry and Ronny, and had them brought into the station for questioning. They had their stories corroborated before Sheriff Lohman could even comprehend his disappointment. The boys had been elsewhere the night of the sisters' disappearance and had not seen either of the girls since. It was another dead lead.

Lorretta lost sleep and wits over the disappearance of her girls. Barbara and Patricia used to sing at Mass every Sunday, and their mother was heartbroken over their absence in the choir. The truth Lorretta could not bring herself to believe was that their sweet voices might never carry through that chapel again.

At this point, Sheriff Lohman was starting to suspect that the girls must have been persuaded somehow to leave their homes and everyone else behind. If they were still alive, he was sure they were traveling with someone, as Lorretta had been insisting the whole time. Sheriff Lohman was so desperate for suspects that he nabbed anyone who had a connection to the case at all. So, when police received an unusual tip from a fifty-three-year-old Chicago native Walter Kranz, claiming he had seen the girls' dead bodies in a dream, officers immediately brought him in for questioning.

Kranz called in anonymously to advise police to look in Santa Fe Park for the girls. Apparently, he had dreamt that they were buried there. But the police weren't buying it, so they attempted to try him for kidnapping and potential murder, given their reasonable suspicion over his claims. Kranz was given a lie detector test three times, but to no avail. His story, albeit strange, was validated as just a dream. The girls were not in Santa Fe Park.

On January 11, the *Chicago Tribune* released an article entitled "Lost Girls' Mother Keeps Brave," marking exactly two weeks since the Grimes sisters had been seen and the last time Lorretta had had a wink of sleep. The staff writer reopened her already sore wounds with the peck of a typewriter.

All that time, Lorretta had a deeply nauseating gut feeling that her daughters had been kidnapped and were being held against their will. Though she had no proof, she insisted that Barbara and Patricia were not the types to run away.

"If someone is holding them, please let them call me," Lorretta pleaded in an interview with the *Tribune*. "I'll forgive them from the bottom of my heart if they let my girls go."

While some might pass off her intuition as colored by grief, Lorretta had a good point. After paying for the film, the girls would have left with just twenty cents in their pockets. Only a few nights previously, Barbara had given her mother the money she had made from a part-time job. She would have surely kept that on her person if she planned to disappear. Lorretta had also just gifted the girls radio headsets for Christmas. Surely, they would have brought them along if they had been preparing to bolt.

To Lorretta, it was proof that her girls didn't steal away; they were stolen.

On January 14, one of Patricia's schoolmates, Sandra Tollstrom, claimed that Patricia had called her home in the middle of the night sounding frightened and scared. Her mother had first picked up the phone around midnight to a voice asking for Sandra. She immediately recognized it as belonging to Patricia, whom she knew had been missing. Patricia was insistent on talking with Sandra, so the mother woke her daughter up and handed the phone over to her. But the line went dead as soon as Sandra put the phone to her ear, never to know if it was really her friend reaching out to her.

On January 18, a Tennessee local claimed the girls had strolled through her store in Memphis, the home of their beloved Elvis. Sheriff Lohman immediately heightened his search in that city, following the theory that the girls had run away, despite Lorretta's adamancy. While it wasn't a stretch, there still wasn't any concrete evidence that the girls had actually embarked on this starstruck journey across the country. Lorretta continued to insist that the girls would never leave home without telling her, but the police seemed resolute to follow any and all leads they possibly had. However, their search in Memphis dissolved within a few days.

On January 19, 1957, Elvis Presley sent out a grave nationwide plea: "If you are good Presley fans, you'll go home and ease your mother's worries." Perhaps he was thinking specifically of the Grimes sisters, who had been missing for twenty-two days. It didn't seem like they would be coming home at all.

But on January 22, the bodies of the two young girls were discovered on the side of German Church Road in Willow Springs, just a couple of miles southwest of their home.

A factory worker named Leonard Prescott spotted these "flesh-colored things" about two hundred feet east of the road along his route to work. Police later identified the remains of Barbara and Patricia half-buried in the snow, a tragic, unjustifiable end to the nearly monthlong search. Their father, Joseph, drove out there that day to identify their bodies.

The girls were found naked and no clothes were discovered nearby. They had been stripped, beaten, and stabbed by their murderers. Barbara had several deep puncture wounds in her chest, seemingly made by some kind of ice pick. It looked as though Patricia had a broken nose and several bruises across her face and chest.

It was obvious the girls had been buried beneath the snow for several days, but their bodies were stiff and slightly decayed, suggesting they had been deceased for nearly a month. Since the bodies were frozen solid, it took a few days for them to thaw out enough for pathologists to perform an autopsy.

Evidence of the girls' last meal was still in their stomachs, indicating that they hadn't even had time to digest it before they were killed. The autopsy confirmed that the Grimes sisters were murdered within hours of leaving the Brighton Theater, either on December 28 or in the early morning of December 29. The puncture wounds were likely inflicted following their deaths, which was, frankly, an odd conclusion.

The autopsy also showed no evidence of carbon monoxide poisoning or any other toxic chemicals. No signs of strangling. No suggestions that either of them had been sexually molested, though the autopsy indicated that Barbara likely had sex, consensually or not, before her death. There were no bullet wounds found anywhere on the bodies, and the autopsy confirmed that the sisters might have died from hypothermia rather than abuse, though they could have corresponded. Their cause of death was officially listed as murder by secondary shock, resulting from exposure to low temperatures.

"My poor babies," Lorretta wept to the *Chicago Tribune* in an interview following the horrible discovery. "Why couldn't they have taken me and let my babies live? If the police had listened to me they would have had the true story half an hour after the girls were missing."

To say that Lorretta was grief-stricken by the loss of her daughters is an understatement. But even after their bodies were found, there was still no justice for the Grimes sisters. Policemen were bewildered by the circumstances of their deaths, the timing of it all, and the continuing influx of false witness sightings, which just confused the investigative process even further. After the murder was confirmed, they received tips that the sisters had been seen stumbling into bars, keeping company with strange men, partying in hotel rooms, and on a bus bound for Memphis, all of which were untrue according to the timeline of their deaths.

On January 28, 1957, Barbara and Patricia Grimes were buried side by side at Holy Sepulchre Cemetery in Worth, Illinois, finally able to rest in peace forever.

In the week following the discovery of the bodies, several witnesses claimed that the Grimes sisters were seen wandering around Chicago between December 29 and January 6 with two young men, one of whom had a keen resemblance to Elvis Presley. While the autopsy had determined the girls were killed within hours of their disappearance, police were desperate to find a man to pin this on, and the dates could have been misleading. Narrowing down their search to one Edward Lee "Bennie" Bedwell, police snatched the twenty-one-year-old up for questioning.

Bedwell told police that he had been with two girls recently, but that they were not the Grimes sisters. He claimed to have been with a friend, Frank, when they were seen with two girls in a tavern on the morning of January 6. They drank the day away in several bars, went to the D & L Restaurant, and then to a film in the 1400 block of Madison Street. The girls apparently ditched him and his pal that night in the middle of the movie. He knew only one of their names as Carol and never spoke to either of them again.

John and Minnie Duros, owners of the D & L Restaurant on Madison Street, where Bedwell sometimes worked as a dishwasher, claimed he and Frank were seen with Barbara and Patricia several times throughout the day on January 6 at the restaurant. Around 6 a.m. the next day, they all came in for a meal and Minnie reported that the girls looked sick, drunk, or doped. It was clear that the men wanted the girls to leave with them, but the older one refused, until the other nudged her into coming along. Minnie claimed that she asked the younger girl why she wouldn't leave the elder girl alone, and she replied that they were sisters. The men left with the girls and Minnie didn't see them again.

There was not enough evidence on the men to charge them. The autopsy showed that the girls had likely died the night of their disappearance and there was no alcohol in their systems, which didn't match the story that could convict Bedwell. There was also no evidence suggesting that the girls had been raped, but it didn't eliminate the possibility that they were sexually assaulted. Nevertheless, Edward Lee Bedwell signed a confession that he had murdered the Grimes sisters.

Later, Bedwell recanted his statement, claiming Chicago police had threatened him, bribed him, even beaten the confession out of him. Since they no longer had anything concrete to tie him to the case, they had to set him free. But some Chicago police believed that Bedwell was the murderer through and through and had calculated a careful response as a cover-up.

As the decades pass, it's questionable whether these reportings were totally accurate or simply used to preserve the girls' reputations in death. In light of 1950s American sentiment, it seems all too clear that police wanted the girls to have died as virgins, and refused to allow that they might have engaged in sexual activity prior to their deaths. This might have been why the police were so keen to believe the story that Bedwell told, rather than what might have been revealed if they really had dug deeper. It might be why authorities ultimately decided to let the story, and him, go— in order to preserve the reputation of these young girls.

The strange murder of the Grimes sisters was retired as a cold case, never to be resolved. The chief investigator for the Cook County coroner's office, Harry Glos, was adamant that the girls were murdered by Edward Bedwell, and in 2013, a retired West Chicago police officer, Raymond Johnson, brought another suspect into the light. Neither, however, has been proved. Police finally gave up any hope of a conclusion that would bring them peace at night, and Lorretta Grimes died years later, never having received justice for her daughters.

But she was adamant to the end that the girls were tough, loved each other fiercely, and would have fought to stay together even through unimaginable horror. "My girls were good girls," she told the *Tribune*, "and I'm sure one would not leave the other even to save her own life."

CHAPTER THIRTEEN

Teresita Basa

The Voice from the Grave

EDGEWATER HOSPITAL WAS A FACILITY ON THE NORTH Side of Chicago in the respected Edgewater neighborhood. Built in 1929, the hospital was the birthplace of notorious serial killer John Wayne Gacy, politician Hillary Rodham Clinton, and many others. The hospital was state of the art for its time, equipped with a helicopter landing pad on the roof and known for its advanced burn-care facilities. Though the hospital is now closed, many regard the abandoned building as cursed, as it once bred the murder of one of its employees.

Teresita Basa was a forty-seven-year-old respiratory therapist at Edgewater Hospital in 1977. She had immigrated to the United States from Dumaguete on the Philippine island of Negros, which had suffered under the weight of a Japanese invasion in the mid-1960s. A member of the Philippine aristocracy, Teresita was fluent in Tagalog and had an accomplished history in concert piano, earning a master's degree in music from Indiana University.

As far as anyone knew, she had no enemies, no reason to be caught in the crossfire of a horrible crime. Perhaps she knew that, too.

On February 21, 1977, firefighters received a distress call from the neighbors of 2740 North Pine Grove Avenue. They smelled and saw smoke and believed a fire had been started in their neighbor's apartment. The fire station came to life that night, its shrieking engines racing across town to extinguish the flames. What the firemen didn't expect was to come face-to-face with one of Chicago's most horrific discoveries to date.

After firefighters rushed up the stairs, burst through the door, and put out the intense flames within minutes, they came across a burning pile of clothes that seemed to be smothering something else. Digging through only a little unveiled the body of Teresita Basa, completely smothered, naked, and burnt to a crisp before their eyes. Her legs were spread wide apart, as if she had been raped, and a kitchen knife protruded from her chest, a murder confirmed.

The firefighters took a closer look at the room before them, not just demolished by flames, but also ransacked to the point of destruction. It was difficult to see what was missing from the room, as nearly everything had been disrupted. When police later arrived at the scene, they realized that evidence was scarce. The killer seemed to have a level of expertise in covering their own tracks, leaving nothing at all behind, including fingerprints.

The only thing police could identify amid the wreckage was a handwritten note tucked away in Teresita's journal: "Get tickets for A.S."

Investigators Joe Stachula and Lee Epplen at the Edgewater police department were assigned to the case. They set out with the only sliver of information they had: Teresita's note. They asked everyone with even a remote connection to Teresita about who the initials might refer to, but no one had the answer for them. Stachula and Epplen worked the frustratingly cold case until it was almost frozen shut. After months of searching, they had no leads, not even a hint of evidence. The newspapers had lost interest a long time ago, as there was nothing fresh in the case. The investigators were completely dumbfounded, utterly at a loss. In the midst of a horror like this, it was terrifying to think that the killer might never be brought to justice.

That was until one ordinary day when the detectives received a call from the Evanston police station inquiring about someone named Allan Showery. The name tugged at an old memory for Stachula, who hoped that he had finally found what he'd been seeking.

According to the Evanston station, Showery was a respiratory technician at Edgewater Hospital, which, Stachula noted, would have put him in close contact with Teresita at work. But the Evanston police had also heard the strangest stories regarding Showery, and they thought Stachula might be interested in hearing what they had to say.

They suggested Stachula get in touch with Dr. Jose Chua. He had contacted them about his wife, Remedios, who also had worked at Edgewater Hospital but had been fired very recently.

Evanston police were vague about why Stachula might find the Chuas' story interesting, but caution aside, he decided to visit them. Stachula went to their home on August 5, 1977, to hear the most unlikely of tales. When he arrived, Dr. Chua ushered him inside and sat him down, preparing him for the unbelievable.

Stachula's grip on logic was tested when Dr. Chua told him that Remedios had been possessed by the spirit of Teresita Basa. Remedios had apparently experienced this phenomenon on three separate occasions, and all very recently. Stranger still, she thought she knew who had killed Teresita.

Overtaken by the voice of Teresita Basa, Remedios Chua pinned the murder on Allan Showery.

Jose Chua, a doctor with a firm belief in logical solutions, was visibly shaken by his wife's transformations. It was evident to him that Remedios had not been her usual self for the past few months, but one night, she was simply bewitched.

Remedios and Jose had been sitting in the living room when Remedios abruptly got up and walked to the bedroom. Sensing that something might be wrong, Jose followed, only to find his wife lying on their bed and blankly staring at the ceiling. When he asked her what was wrong, she spoke in a low, strange voice that was unlike her own. Like Teresita, Remedios also spoke Tagalog, her native language, but when the words spilled from her mouth, Jose didn't recognize the inflections in her tone.

As a medical man, Jose was used to strange and unexplained miracles, but this was something else entirely. He cautiously asked her name, just to find out if his wife was even conscious.

Remedios looked at him and whispered in Tagalog, "*Ako'y* [I am] Teresita Basa."

Jose was confused and slightly frightened. He had no knowledge of this Teresita Basa or why his wife was suddenly impersonating her. He pressed her for more information, and Remedios told him that Teresita had been murdered. This was too much for Jose, who tried to wake his wife from her stupor, but it took a half hour before Remedios was back in her usual form, incognizant of anything that had happened. She was, however, very thirsty.

Discussing it together later, the Chuas both decided it would be better not to come forward with what Jose had just witnessed. But then it happened a second time.

Remedios fell into a transformative state a few weeks later, and Jose must have been terrified at this point. But he was also a little more prepared and proceeded to question his wife, ever so cautiously, about what was happening to her. Remedios went on to explain exactly how she, as Teresita, was murdered, down to the very last detail. Remedios divulged to Jose that Showery had stolen from Teresita during the raid, including precious jewelry, something of which even the police, at this point, were unaware.

It was only when Remedios was overtaken by the voice of Teresita a third time that Jose asked who her killer might be.

"Allan Showery," Remedios said. Jose knew that name. Remedios had worked with Showery at the hospital, and while they knew each other fairly well, they were definitely not friends.

Jose claimed he had not even heard of Teresita or her death before his wife started speaking as her. Now Remedios was earnestly claiming that Showery was the killer.

That's when Jose knew they had to go to the police.

Stachula was very wary of the story, but after so many months of searching fruitlessly for the killer, his only option was to speak with Remedios. She refused to talk to him, stating only that it had been traumatic for both her and Jose to go through this unexplained experience. So Stachula pressed Jose for more information about what his wife had said during these transformations and what she knew of Teresita Basa at work.

Remedios was hardly even acquainted with Teresita, and they rarely, if ever, saw each other at the hospital. She did, however, know Allan Showery.

Though police initially assumed it was a rape-murder situation, test results showed that Teresita was a virgin when she was killed, and so Stachula made it a point to ask Jose what his wife had said about that. Remedios was on track with the story, though—she claimed that Teresita had only been stabbed. According to Remedios, Teresita had asked Showery to come over after work to fix her television. He did so, only to knock her unconscious, kill her, and rob her apartment.

All of this information was taken at the word of Jose and Remedios Chua. Stachula never saw Teresita's ghost overtake Remedios. All he knew was that he had a name and, therefore, a lead, and he had to follow it, regardless of the ridiculous circumstances in which he stumbled across it.

Stachula confronted Allan Showery in his home, where he lived with his girlfriend, at 630 West Shubert Avenue on August 11, 1977. He asked if Showery would be able to come down to the station for questioning, and the suspect was compliant.

When Stachula asked if Showery had been at Teresita's apartment on the night she died, Showery first denied but then admitted to being there. Stachula used the new piece of information about stolen jewelry to confront Showery, who said that he knew nothing about it. Police later found that Showery's girlfriend, Yanka Kamluk, was in possession of some of the jewelry, and was even wearing one of the items when they confronted her. It was a pearl cocktail ring, and Yanka told police that Showery had gifted her jewelry as a belated Christmas present, sometime toward the end of February. Relatives of Teresita identified the ring and another jade pendant in Yanka's possessions as having belonged to the slain woman, and it was enough to arrest Allan Showery for robbery.

It was only then that Showery added another piece of information to his story: Teresita had given those pieces to him as a generous financial offer, he said, but he clearly didn't use them to dig himself out of debt. All of this evidence was enough to put him on trial for murder, arson, and robbery, and Showery was in for a few years of legal weight on his shoulders. Perhaps under pressure by the police or simply because he felt his hands were tied, Allan Showery admitted to the killing before being placed on trial.

This avalanche of evidence also saved the Chuas from being tried in connection to the murder. After all, they knew so much. Assuming the voice from the grave act was just that, an act, the Chuas certainly did have a lot of information on hand, enough for suspicions to rise. But at the end of it all, police were positive that the Chuas were not connected to the murder at all. They may have known more than they chose to let on, but police were willing to forgive how the information was received as long as they could put someone behind bars.

Showery was thrown into Cook County Jail while he awaited his trial.

The trial began in a flurry and lasted from August 1977 through February of the next year. Thirty-three witnesses were called before a jury of eight men and four women. Showery was assigned defense lawyers William Swano and Daniel Radakovich against prosecutors Thomas Organ and Lee Schoen.

Jose Chua was called to testify and explained how his wife was overtaken by the spirit of Teresita. Whether or not the judge believed this strange story, it was allowed in court and both the defense attorneys and the prosecutors relied on it heavily.

Swano made the point that Remedios Chua might have been faking these supposed supernatural episodes because she was in the midst of being fired when they happened. He argued that she was probably upset or confused, and wasn't thinking straight. Perhaps it was a psychotic episode, he argued, and Showery was just caught in the crossfire.

Or perhaps she was thinking all too clearly. Maybe she knew something about Allan Showery's actions and was too afraid to come forward without a mask to hide behind.

Spiritual possession clearly did the trick, even if it was a strange avenue to take.

Organ argued that police didn't truly have grounds upon which to arrest Showery, since the method by which he was named was totally fantastical. But criminal court judge Frank W. Barbaro rejected this line of reasoning and the trial went on with the evidence stacked high against Showery.

Swano and Radakovich contended that Showery had been elsewhere on the night of the murder: kicking back with his buddies, shooting darts and drinking in his neighbor's home. Showery's girlfriend, Yanka, was brought in as a witness for him, but Organ and Schoen tore into her with information from her previous statement—namely, that she had been out shopping and Showery had been at home doing electrical work on the night of Teresita's murder. Yanka didn't stand a chance.

As the trial went on, Showery tried to change his story and became increasingly more desperate to prove his innocence. He claimed that police had tricked him into confessing and that they would have jailed his pregnant girlfriend if he didn't admit to the murder. He told the jury he was "just kidding" when he confessed to the crime, which seems like a desperate attempt at backtracking all of the conflicting information he had fed police.

It was Organ's final remarks that sealed Showery's fate. Whether or not Remedios's spirit overtaking was true, it didn't matter. "What does matter is that the information checked out," Organ said to a contemplative courtroom.

He ended the courtroom session by holding the murder weapon high into the air, waving it at Showery as he shouted, "You weren't kidding when you plunged this knife into Teresita Basa's chest!"

In spite of all the signs pointing directly at Showery, the whole series of events ended in a mistrial with a deadlocked jury. This was good news for Showery. It meant he could walk free if the judge decided to dismiss charges. It could have ended in an agreement with strict terms, or even just delayed his punishment for a rescheduled trial.

Instead, Allan Showery admitted—on February 22, 1979, just one day after the two-year anniversary of Basa's death, and against the wishes of his lawyers—that he did, in fact, murder Teresita. He confessed that he had visited Teresita on the night of her death and knocked her out. But as for Teresita's apparently defiled body, Showery was adamant that he only staged the sexual assault. He claimed to have stolen what he could, including the jewelry, and lit a fire in the apartment. And above all—or, more accurately, far beneath it all—Showery confessed to the murder of Teresita Basa. Judge Barbaro sentenced Showery to fourteen years at the Stateville Correctional Center near Joliet on charges of murder, robbery, and arson.

Though it failed to make a difference in the end, the Chuas were brought into the courtroom as witnesses for the defense. It was possible that Remedios Chua was afraid of Showery and what he could do, but if that had been the case, letting him walk free could only result in more harm done. Remedios might have thought the method of possession would soften her accusation, but she also would have been afraid of what could happen when Showery realized that she knew the truth, regardless of how she found it.

While "the voice from the grave" may have fooled some supernatural believers, it's a bit too easily constructed. Remedios knew Showery, and they both knew Teresita, as they all worked at the same hospital together. It wasn't as if someone totally irrelevant had possessed Remedios. They were colleagues. Apparently, Showery had made several complaints about Remedios to Human Resources at work but also harassed her on multiple occasions, even going so far as to make a prank phone call to her at home. Remedios and Showery disliked each other. Perhaps she knew something about Showery's plans to kill Teresita or, if it wasn't premeditated, perhaps she saw or gained insight after it happened and wasn't sure how to express what she knew to the police. The supernatural possession just may have been a defense mechanism kicking in to save herself from his wrath.

"To this day, I'm not quite sure whether I believe how the information was obtained," Investigator Stachula said to the *Chicago Tribune* on March 5, 1978. "Nonetheless, everything here is completely true."

Allan Showery served just four years in prison; he was paroled in 1983 on good behavior. It's not clear where he lives today, if he is still alive.

Remedios and Jose Chua lived a long life together. They helped publish a book on their version of the events, *The Voice from the Grave* by *Chicago Tribune* reporters John O'Brien and Edward Baumann, but disliked the publicity that it brought them for years after. Jose passed away in 2002, but Remedios may still be alive today. As far as history knows, no more voices from the grave ever bothered her again.

CHAPTER FOURTEEN

Flight 191

The Deadliest Plane Crash in Chicago History

ALMOST TWO DECADES AFTER THE EVENTS OF 9/11, AMER-
icans still remember exactly where they were when the twin
towers of the World Trade Center in New York City fell. The
act that sparked a war is a morbid reminder of the unspoken
dangers of flying, inspiring a fear so far-reaching that security measures nationwide were adjusted to prevent anything
like that happening again.

The nation's most tragic aviation accident not caused by
an act of terrorism happened within Illinois, not far from
the outskirts of Chicago. It was an accident that shook the
nation, likewise causing a widespread unnerved feeling about
ever taking to the skies again.

American Airlines Flight 191 took off from O'Hare
International Airport on Friday, May 25, 1979, at 3:04 p.m.
The flight was scheduled to land in Los Angeles later that
day. Many were going home and others taking a warm vacation from the Windy City to the City of Angels. Unfortunately, no winged spirits showed mercy that day. Instead, the

Angel of Death appeared and hundreds of lives were lost in the resulting crash.

The air traffic control tower radioed the pilot, readying the crew for the impending flight. "American 191. Turn right heading 330. Cleared for takeoff 32R. No delay."

Flight 191 started roaring its way down the runway. But when it reached takeoff speed, the primary engine came loose and was ripped from the underwing of the plane, a McDonnell Douglas DC-10. The wing was damaged, along with the major hydraulic systems, but by then, the plane was already off the ground, and nothing could have been done to steer it back to safety. The plane was in the air for only thirty-one seconds before tilting 30, then 60, then 90 degrees to the left, hurtling almost belly-up back toward the ground. Flight 191 plummeted sharply to the left and crashed hard into a field off Touhy Avenue, just 4,600 feet past the runway edge.

The plane instantly burst into flames, consuming the people on board who hadn't been killed on impact. Bystanders, even those miles away, saw the enormous plume of black smoke rippling from the crash site. Ambulances and first responders rushed to the scene, only to find that their services were not needed. No one had survived. The aircraft crew of 13, plus 258 passengers and 2 more on the ground, had lost their lives to the fatal crash.

Removal of the bodies began shortly after firefighters from Elk Grove Township and Des Plaines found nothing but a gaping hole in the earth and fragments of the aircraft. The crash of Flight 191 was and still remains the deadliest aviation accident in US history.

Lessons learned from this horrifying crash helped improve aviation security in the decades to come. Maintenance practices were standardized going forward to prevent oversights and human error. Military fighter planes have always undergone extensive maintenance checks before taking flight. But post–Flight 191, civilian aircraft started receiving the same attention. Since Flight 191, 9/11, and several Boeing 737 Max crashes, American flight safety has advanced to ensure the security of its passengers. Boeing 737s were taken off the market in 2019. In general, security measures have increased and aircrafts are now triple-checked to ensure all pieces are working in tandem for smooth sailing through the skies.

Flight 191 has a memorial wall in the Des Plaines Park District, open to those who still mourn the loss of their loved ones.

PART III

STRANGE BEGINNINGS TO CHICAGO'S OLDEST LANDMARKS

Exterior view of the Iroquois Theatre the day after the fire, December 31, 1903. CHICAGO HISTORY MUSEUM, ICHI-070895; CHARLES R. CLARK, PHOTOGRAPHER

CHAPTER FIFTEEN

Lincoln Park

The Skeletal History That Lies Beneath

LINCOLN PARK IS ONE OF CHICAGO'S GREATEST OUTDOOR attractions, a vivacious landscape of wild greenery and delicate ponds, through which visitors may venture by serene boardwalk. Housing the only zoo within city limits, the park welcomes more than twenty million visitors every year. Though Lincoln Park exists today as a beautiful sanctuary, tucked away from the restless noise of the city, many are unaware that more than twelve thousand corpses are buried beneath the grasslands.

Before Chicago was incorporated as a city in 1837, Lincoln Park was an unoccupied green space on the north end of civilization, lush with overgrown foliage and continuously hydrated by nearby Lake Michigan. The state of Illinois granted the little town of Chicago two permits to set aside land for cemeteries on the North and South sides, and so City Cemetery was established near the lakeshore in 1835. That small plot of land covers the very south end of what locals know as Lincoln Park today.

The first corpses were buried in City Cemetery in 1843, but soon, there would be many more to follow. Chicago was struck by its first major cholera outbreak in 1849, a disease that took the lives of many people through 1854. Due to a rapidly expanding population and an increase in illness-related deaths, the cemetery was filling up quickly and required expansion in order to accommodate the extra bodies. But the city made a mistake when it encroached on the farm of Jacob Milliman. Whether by accident or on purpose is lost to history, but for the next fifteen years, the bodies of disease-ridden Chicagoans were buried in that sliver of Milliman's land. The original Millimans died before an attorney representing their land brought the case to the Supreme Court, which ruled that the city had acquired the land illegally. That section of the cemetery was eventually given back to the surviving Milliman family members, resulting in the first of many disinterments in the area in 1865.

The last lots available in City Cemetery were sold to Chicago residents in May 1859. Rosehill Cemetery opened in August 1859 as Chicago's first rural cemetery, making it the perfect place to accept the newly departed. Graceland Cemetery was established the next year, along with the Catholic Calvary Cemetery. The land for Oak Woods Cemetery was cleared out in 1853 but did not start accepting bodies until 1860.

As Chicago residents moved out into the northern neighborhoods, they were faced with the sickening stench of rotting corpses from the nearby City Cemetery. Health risks were a concern, too. People of that time believed that corpses give off noxious air called miasma, and locals who lived close to these mortal remains would breathe in toxins. Though folklore today prompts the superstitious to hold their breath while passing a cemetery because they may inhale lost souls, logic of the 1850s suggested not breathing to avoid the unhealthy air.

With the gravesites being so close to Lake Michigan, residents also worried that their drinking water would be polluted. Their desire for a public park grew as quickly as the population did, and with the area surrounding City Cemetery being so close to the waterfront, it seemed the perfect place to leave natural for the next century. In 1863, city officials dubbed the northern half of the unscathed land as Cemetery Park, renamed Lake Park in 1864. The great expanse north of City Cemetery was officially named Lincoln Park in 1865 after President Abraham Lincoln was assassinated.

But bodies still remained under the earth very near to the park, in the small stretch of City Cemetery. Families were given the option to move their loved ones to a more peaceful environment, away from the bustle of the urban streets now surrounding the cemetery, and many of them permitted the remains to be unearthed and reburied in the newer burial grounds. With the Milliman land being the first to disrupt the sleep of the dead in 1865, many other graves were disinterred in the following years. But not all of them.

Chicago had split the burials of its citizens into sections: the potter's field, the Catholic cemetery, the Jewish cemetery, and the general City Cemetery. The poor were laid to rest in the potter's field, where baseball diamonds have become a staple of the modern Lincoln Park's activities. Though the city had prohibited any new burials in City Cemetery, this did not include the potter's fields and private lots reserved for the religious. Many of the Confederate soldiers imprisoned at nearby Camp Douglas passed away from cholera and also were buried in the potter's field, dubbed the "rebel graves" during the Civil War. Historians estimate that over 15,212 were buried in the potter's field and private sections from 1862 to 1865.

When the Great Chicago Fire broke out in 1871, thousands of people fled to the wild expanse of Lincoln Park for safety, only to watch the flames ransack what remained of the potter's field section of the graveyard. Wooden headstones were engulfed and even stone markers were cracked and soiled with soot. The great inferno stretched all the way to Fullerton Avenue, but the flames weren't the only force that proved devastating to the park. The masses of humans trampling the gravesites disrupted many of the remains buried in shallow graves. Luckily, torrents of rain eventually extinguished the flames for good, but not before the Great Fire had caused irreparable damage to both the city and its dead.

Though the last of the graves should have been moved in 1872 to Rosehill Cemetery and other rural burial grounds, park records show that disinterment continued until as late as 1887, leaving a lot of room for miscalculation. The estimated number of individuals still buried in Lincoln Park was a little murky and city workers may have ceased the unearthing of bodies a little too soon, not knowing that there were several thousand still buried because their grave markers had been destroyed in the inferno. There is no existing official record confirming that every single body was unearthed.

Over the almost century and a half that has transpired since, construction workers have accidentally excavated human remains, scattered bones, and unmarked coffins nearly every time they start digging in Lincoln Park, including while building the parking garage for the Chicago History Museum and expanding the Lincoln Park Zoo. The Chicago History Museum was built as the Chicago Historical Society in 1896, following the original building's destruction in the Great Chicago Fire. The current construction exists on the southwest end of Lincoln Park, exactly on top of where City Cemetery was originally formed.

Over the course of just twenty-five years, the southern fifty-seven acres of Lincoln Park's City Cemetery became the tomb for more than thirty-five thousand citizens. Though historical reports of disinterment are unclear as to the total number that were moved, it's estimated that more than twelve thousand bodies still remain beneath the park, forever lost without their headstones.

Couch Place Alley's namesake and one of the first millionaires to live in Chicago, Ira Couch, was entombed in a grand mausoleum on the south side of City Cemetery in 1858. The city never moved the massive vault for one of several reasons: it may have been too heavy, but it also would have cost $3,000 to deracinate and relocate. Couch might not be alone in there, either, possibly buried alongside several of his family members, the number of which is widely debated. The Couch crypt stands tall and solemn today, protected by the park district, as the only remaining evidence that Chicago's ancestors once slept beneath the soil of Lincoln Park.

CHAPTER SIXTEEN

The Iroquois Theatre Fire

The Alley of Death and Mutilation

WHAT IS CURRENTLY KNOWN AS CHICAGO'S GREENEST Alley was once a gravesite of unimaginable horrors.

Glittering like the *Titanic* must have in its day, the Iroquois Theatre was ready to take on a century of theatrical phenomena before its utter obliteration. Though it took only five months to complete, the cost to build the palatial playhouse totaled in the millions, a gasp-worthy feat in its day. It might have made the Second City second to none.

But the Iroquois Theatre stood for less than a year, ran a single show, and held a single audience's attention for a single night. It also caused the deaths of more than six hundred people.

On December 30, 1903, *Mr. Bluebeard* was debuting at the Iroquois Theatre. It was a musical comedy brought to Chicago from New York City, following the story of a man who murdered his wives and hid their bodies in closets: gruesome even for a dark comedy. But that wasn't the only horror to befall the eighteen hundred audience members that evening.

Though many regular folk attended this first showing, there were a few shimmering celebrities in the mix as well. Among the honored guests were John G. Shedd, the future famed proprietor of Chicago's Shedd Aquarium, and Charles Plamondon, an official of the Chicago Board of Education. But despite their differences, all were there to witness the spectacle of what could have been the most influential stage of all time.

At this point in history, theaters still used colorful scenery flats, or backdrops, to depict the landscape and set the stage, which, unfortunately, were not "absolutely fireproof," contrary to the playbill's boast. The Iroquois Theatre held approximately 280 of them suspended from wooden shafts above the main stage.

As the second act of the show was well underway, a stage light shorted and caught one of the backdrops on fire. Kilfyre powder was used by the crew to try and subdue the flames, but since the fire had caught from the top and was spreading downward, the powder was useless against the quickly growing inferno.

It was at this point that the crowd realized what was going on and started to panic. The star of the show, Eddie Foy, did his best to announce what was happening and send the audience quietly outside. But who is ever calm in the midst of disaster?

A massive wave of people pushed against the back wall of the theater, desperate to find their escape. The exit doors were not clearly marked, as they might have been today, and were thus harder to identify. But once people did realize where they were, their hearts sank as they figured out that all the doors were locked with a special kind of European latch unfamiliar to Chicagoans. Though there were a few quick thinkers in the room who could undo the lock, the doors were built so that they swung inward instead of outward. With the force of the crowd pressing in upon them, it wasn't even possible to open the doors.

The asbestos fire curtain did exist in this era, but as the crew tried to lower it to subdue the flames, it snagged on the lighting equipment and fell only halfway down, leaving plenty of flame open to escape into the theater. The Iroquois had also been built with a skylight that could be opened in case of a fire to let the heat rise and allow the smoke to clear out that way. But to the crewmembers' horror, it had been bolted shut and could not be opened.

The crew was able to escape out the back door, but once that was opened, it sent in a gust of freezing air that only fanned the flames, sending them outward into the seats.

It was a custom to keep the upper-level area locked once the house was full, as upper-level purchasers were often not as wealthy as those who sat below. They wanted to keep stray people from sneaking onto the ground floor, but in this case, it proved fatal. Everyone on the upper level was trapped inside by the locked metal accordion doors keeping them away from the ground floor.

Since it was the middle of winter in Chicago, and thus a frigid wasteland, the fire escapes were all frozen, unable to be lowered to the ground. Couch Place Alley loomed far below, but the flames were catching up and people had to make desperate decisions to save their own lives.

Unfortunately, this plan worked only for some. The first few people to jump from the fire escapes fell to their deaths in the alley, but more people kept on coming. Some sources claim the pile of bodies reached six feet high, a monument to the tragic events that happened that night.

The apartment building next door came to the rescue for some, with residents shoving two-by-four ladders and wooden planks out their windows and across Couch Place Alley to the Iroquois Theatre. Many patrons made their escape this way, crawling slowly to safety, but others teetered on these precarious ledges until they ultimately lost their balance and fell, too.

The majority of the deaths happened in the playhouse, but Couch Place Alley held too many bodies to count by the time the fire had subsided. Though the entire event concluded within half an hour, it caused unmitigated damage and claimed more than six hundred lives.

The true mystery of Couch Place Alley and the Iroquois Theatre fire is in the safety measures. What we know is that a stage light supposedly shorted, the fire curtain snagged, the skylight was bolted shut, the fire escapes were frozen, and all of the exits were unlabeled, locked, and opened inward. While it's possible that these features were just overlooked by building constructors, they seem crucial to ensuring that everyone in the theater could escape safely. In fact, that's a lot of neglect, not just a simple mistake. True, many safety precautions that we have today were implemented post-fire, but after the Great Chicago Fire in 1871, most businesses and venues made sure that their buildings were flame-proof, terrified of another mishap. And yet the Iroquois Theatre was basically unfinished when it opened to the public, leaving the audience, cast, and crew dangerously vulnerable to a disaster.

It turns out that prior to opening night, *Fireproof* magazine had sent an editor to inspect the Iroquois Theatre. William Clendenin had concluded that the exits were inadequate, the wood trim would certainly cause flames to spread quickly, and a stage draft shaft was missing from the design. Not only that, but the Chicago Fire Department and Engine Company 13 both made appearances at the theater before opening night and expressed their concern for the lack of safety measures in place at the Iroquois. They noted that the fire exits were concealed and that there was no fire alarm system in place, definitely no sprinkler, no backstage appliances to help subdue a fire, and so many more violations of fire safety code at the time. Kilfyre powder was the only adequate weapon against the flames in sight, and it had next to no impact at the time of the tragedy.

Though all of this was reported back to the fire department, it went unresolved. The theater owners were aware of the issues at the time of construction and simply never bothered to address them. Unfortunately, that resulted in hundreds of lives lost at the expense of a few hundred dollars.

The *Chicago Tribune* dubbed Couch Place Alley "The Alley of Death and Mutilation" when the story first broke. There couldn't have been a more fitting title. While nothing occupied the site of the Iroquois Theatre for decades, the Oriental Theatre—renamed the James M. Nederlander Theatre in 2019—eventually replaced the skeletal structure in

1926 without any plaque, monument, or mention at all that a massive tragedy took place there.

Though Couch Place Alley is a strange name, there is nothing sinister about it, as far as research goes. Brothers Ira and James Couch owned Chicago's first brick building—constructed before the Great Chicago Fire—the original Tremont Hotel. The alley was named after them.

Ira and James Couch practically created the Loop. They were rich hotel owners and eventually bought out the land and property around them, selling it off to local buyers. Ira was one of the wealthiest men in Chicago with only two above him: city mayor William B. Ogden and publisher and eventual mayor John "Long John" Wentworth.

Ira Couch was buried in Lincoln Park within a massive mausoleum. Any local resident knows the solemn, somehow intimidating, capital letters imprinted in the stone, simply reading "COUCH," though it's doubtful that anyone realizes the connection between this far-away tomb and the Loop's Couch Place Alley.

CHAPTER SEVENTEEN

The Green Mill

Mob Mentality at Chicago's Top Jazz Club

THE GREEN MILL COCKTAIL LOUNGE—OR THE GREEN Mill Cafe, as it was originally billed—enveloped the Uptown streets in an emerald glow every night. The neon signage enchanted people from all over town who glided into the nightclub to enjoy the finest cabaret the city had ever seen.

Residing at 4802 North Broadway Avenue, the Green Mill cultivated the music scene in Uptown and, therefore, the very essence of culture and community throughout Chicago's North Side neighborhood. But before the Green Mill was a Second City institution spilling classic jazz out onto the block, it was just the closest bar to the neighboring Graceland and Saint Boniface cemeteries. Opened in 1907 as Pop Morse's Roadhouse, the bar and beer garden sheltered mourners while they toasted their departed loved ones. Then, under new ownership, the Green Mill became an illustrious nightclub and a hideaway for the Chicago Outfit.

When real estate owner Tom Chamales purchased the property in 1910, he went through a rebranding period. He wanted to allude to the famous Moulin Rouge but knew that naming a bar "Red Mill" might not have the best connotation. Just a few neighborhoods south of Uptown, drunk men stumbled through the dimly lit streets of the red-light district to find a brothel, and the new owner didn't want to be associated with that scene. Instead, he named the place the Green Mill Gardens, just a slight nod to the Parisian cabaret. Chamales later went on to build the Riviera Theatre, also a modern-day Chicago staple, right down the street.

Just before Prohibition became law, the Green Mill was quintessential for all sorts of nightly entertainment, from singing groups to comedy acts to dance numbers, but the greatest of these was jazz music. A soothing new musical genre that no one had ever heard before was brought from the South to Chicago, attracting vocalists, vaudevillians, and artists from all over town to the enthralling nightclub. When the Uptown Theatre was built in 1925 just across the street, an even more dramatic crowd descended upon the area, which only amplified the success of the Green Mill. Regulars at the bar included effervescent thespians who performed shows in the neighborhood. Even Charlie Chaplin stopped by once.

He wasn't the only famed star to visit, either. The Green Mill played host to many celebrities of the day, including classic jazz talents Von Freeman, Franz Jackson, and Wilbur Campbell. The Green Mill helped develop the illustrious careers of singers Billie Holiday, Al Jolson, Anita O'Day, and Helen Morgan, and was even visited by cabaret icon Texas Guinan when she spent a brief time in Chicago, 1928 to 1930.

Everyone knew that the Green Mill was the place to be during Prohibition. The illegality of public consumption didn't stop anybody; most of the jazz crowd hid their bootlegged gin in a hip flask and drank freely throughout the night. Years later, empty bottles were found slipped between booth seats, the evidence tucked away for decades. Booze was the strongest bonding element of the era, especially after the troops came home. Everybody drank to forget the war.

Chamales eventually leased the speakeasy to a member of Al Capone's Chicago Outfit, Jack "Machine Gun" McGurn, in an under-the-table exchange. Chicago's most notorious gangster was a frequent visitor to the trendiest club in the city during the Prohibition era. Capone even had his own table, perpetually reserved in the corner of the bar. Since he was technically encroaching on "Bugs" Moran's North Side territory, his booth was angled in a way that Capone could face both entryways and always keep a vigilant eye out for trouble.

Whenever the mob boss stopped by, the bandleader knew to stop whatever he was playing and immediately start into George Gershwin's "Rhapsody in Blue," Capone's favorite musical number. The Green Mill was useful to the Chicago gangster for one specific purpose: to move bootlegged alcohol. A series of tunnels was carved out beneath the Green Mill, originally used to transport coal to the bar's boilers, but Capone organized for booze to be smuggled below the bar while alcohol remained illegal from 1920 to 1933. Historians also believe the tunnels were his preferred method of escape when the cops came lurking around the speakeasy.

Once, a cabaret singer named Joseph Lewis intended to leave the Green Mill for a higher-paid opportunity at a joint called the Rendezvous Cafe. He was making only $600 a week at the Green Mill and wasn't about to turn down the $1,000 offer. But then he was approached by "Machine Gun" McGurn, who threatened him, saying he would "take him for a ride" if he tried to leave the Green Mill. At the time, no one knew for sure that McGurn had partial ownership of the Green Mill, but many suspected it. Lewis thought no one would take that much interest in his employment opportunities unless they had some kind of involvement, and for months he was terrified of whatever fate would befall him.

A few months later, Lewis was found beaten, bloodied, and bruised in his dressing room at the Commonwealth Hotel, which was located near the lake, at 2757 North Pine Grove Avenue. He was unable to identify his assailants, let alone nod his head yes or no to initial questions. Though his stab wounds might have been enough to kill him, he survived and told his side of the story to *Chicago Tribune* reporters. The thugs were never caught, and Lewis eventually returned to the Green Mill to start up a comedy act. Though it was never proven, many, including Lewis, believed that Capone's gang was behind the attack. When Lewis's story became the inspiration for the 1957 film *The Joker Is Wild*, Frank Sinatra was cast in the leading role and paid several visits to the Green Mill to rehearse and grab a drink between takes.

After World War II, the Green Mill fell into ruin. It no longer served as a secret haven for imbibers, but for the next forty years it attracted day-drinkers and drug abusers instead. Though the air was still thick with historical influence, its glory days were clearly over, or so everyone thought.

The Green Mill was slightly renamed when it was bought out in 1986 by Dave Jemilo, who revived the speakeasy-turned-dive-bar into a shining beacon of American jazz once again. Still a staple of Chicago today, the Green Mill Cocktail Lounge is no longer controlled by the Mafia, but those interested in the darker side of Chicago history will find the old speakeasy fascinating.

CHAPTER EIGHTEEN

Lottie's Pub

The Secret Rathskeller Owned by Chicago's Intersex Heroine

IN THE MIDST OF PROHIBITION, SPEAKEASIES BEGAN CROPping up all over Chicago's underground vice world, but none so unique as Lottie's Pub. Originally operated under the name Zagorski's Tavern as a neighborhood grocery store with a full bar, Lottie's Pub is counted among the quintessential Chicago bars that dotted mob history. Beneath the regular store patrons' feet was a pocket of vice, a secret rathskeller, to which the most corrupted of characters would flock. And their fearless leader? An LGBTQ+ icon whose story would transcend historical bias.

The building opened in 1928, originally as a grocery store, but that was before its prime. The store was taken over in May 1934 by an intersex woman named Lottie Zagorski, a strongly connected, intimidating, six-foot-tall figure who converted one side of the building into a full-service bar. Whether Lottie—born Walter, but known widely by her feminine name—was transgender or just liked to dress in drag is unclear, but what is known is that Lottie was well-respected in her community.

Locals in the Shakespeare District of Bucktown, where the tavern existed, knew her as charming, confident, and generous. Lottie ran her grocery store as smoothly as possible and often handed out cash to local kids who passed through for a snack. Most of the community had heard the rumors that the store's secret basement tavern played host to mob meetups but were happy to leave well enough alone. The less they knew, the safer they were when police eventually came asking questions. Lottie had to have been extremely well-connected to dangerous criminals in order to maintain the silence of an entire community.

Soon after Lottie took over the joint, Zagorski's Tavern shot up on the list of mobster hangout spots. The basement rathskeller offered a level of anonymity that the Loop-area speakeasies couldn't, being so far from downtown. Located a little off the grid like that allowed Lottie to run a highly secret, underground network of poker games, off-track betting, mob meetings, strip shows, and other vices. While Lottie wasn't a gangster herself, she often oversaw mobster payoffs and illegal gambling in the rathskeller. Even city officials crept through to finalize underhanded monetary deals with gang members.

From 1933 to 1947, Mayor Edward Kelly ran one of the most corrupt political organizations that Chicago has ever seen. The previous seat-holder, Anton Cermak, had been killed in an assassination attempt against the president-elect at the time, Franklin D. Roosevelt, so Kelly was sworn in after Cook County Democratic Party chairman Patrick A.

Nash made sure to put in a good word. Together, the two formed the "Kelly-Nash Machine," which controlled the Democratic Party in Chicago. This meant that gangsters and other corrupt individuals could sway the minds of politicians if they offered money, power, or other rewards, and politicians could get mobsters to do their bidding in exchange for immunity.

Technically, Kelly and Nash were among the most progressive politicians Chicago had ever seen—allowing African American men to have a say in the political process for the first time in history—but their apathy regarding the violence that dominated the city streets was concerning. Kelly wasn't necessarily corrupt himself, but it would be negligent to ignore how vice went undetected in his own political party. Organized crime was ramping up during this period in time, and the gangster era was in full swing. People noticed all of that. Lottie noticed, too.

Zagorski's Tavern used to run strip shows every Saturday night in the secret rathskeller, which gave the working women, who otherwise would have had low-paying jobs, a reasonable wage. The whole place was an escape from the stifling orthodox attitudes of the outside world, a shelter where vice and debauchery liberated the outlaws who refused to operate under restrained lifestyles. It also gave hope to those who existed somewhere outside the norm of society—a world where differences could be accepted as beautiful and independence was celebrated.

Lottie had an associate, Andy "the Greek" Lochious, who ran the gambling operation in the rathskeller. Andy was linked to the mob and could provide invaluable connections to Chicago's underworld. This helped Lottie become famous in the gangster community, and infamous within her neighborhood. The two managed this secret affair for three decades, drawing celebrity mobsters and even famous writers, like Nelson Algren, to the tavern. Algren's money supported much of the gambling bets, and he won big nearly every time.

The magic came to an end in the mid-1960s, however, when the political climate shifted in favor of cleaning up the streets. In 1967, the Federal Bureau of Investigation and the Internal Revenue Service performed a raid on Zagorski's Tavern, finally discovering the hidden rathskeller beneath the innocent-looking grocery store. They found a treasure trove of illegal racehorse bet slips and scratch sheets, more than ten thousand football parlay cards, and plenty of 16-gauge shotguns. Lottie and Andy were arrested on charges of illegal bookkeeping and having loads of paraphernalia on-site at the tavern. But that wasn't the end for Lottie.

Within hours of her arrest, the cops who arrested Lottie Zagorski received dozens of calls from politicians and businessmen, with reputations so far untainted, who vouched for Lottie's character. It must have been a risky move, but it terrified the police more than the gangster world ever could. Lottie Zagorski could not be touched because she had touched too many lives.

Lottie died on October 1, 1973, of natural causes, never having been charged in connection with the crimes that ran amok in the rathskeller. Under new management, Zagorski's Tavern was renamed Lottie's Pub in 1986 to commemorate the legacy of the tavern owner Bucktown couldn't help but love.

Corner bars in the middle of a Chicago neighborhood used to be more common than they are now. The few still standing have been around for nearly a century or more at this point in time, but there are hardly any new corner taverns being built today. Lottie's Pub still stands in the Shakespeare District of Bucktown on the corner of Cortland and Winchester.

CHAPTER NINETEEN

Cabrini Homes

Systemic Racism and Gang Violence in Chicago's First Slum

THE NEAR NORTH SIDE OF CHICAGO IS HARDLY KNOWN AS a gang-centric neighborhood in the twenty-first century, but it used to be. Chicago's first slum was known as "Little Hell" from as early as the 1860s, infamous for its constant bloodshed. The city of Chicago noticed this upswing in violence, but its solution to the issue was far worse. This notorious neighborhood block became the grounds for the disreputable Cabrini low-rises in 1942 and forever changed gang history in Chicago.

Irish immigrants first migrated to the Near North Side in the 1850s and were quickly swept up into the manufacturing industries that were booming there. The nickname "Little Hell" was first born of the gas flames that ignited the skies from atop the Peoples Gas Light and Coke Company building, but it turned out to be all too fitting for the underground gambling dens and brothels that developed beneath those streets at the same time. In 1860, Michael Cassius

McDonald assailed the ranks within these vice pockets and created the Irish Mob, using his political connections to keep his operations secretive and effective.

In the 1880s, Sicilian immigrants started to settle into the Near North Side, too, causing tension between the Irish and the incoming Italians. Turf wars quickly unfurled between Irish and Italian gangs, but there was no victory to be had on either side. Death was a plague that rapidly infected the Near North Side, birthing both the Chicago Irish Mob and the Chicago Italian Mafia at the turn of the century.

At the time, the Italian Mafia had a subgroup of Black Hand extortionists who would send anonymous notes to select individuals, usually those who opposed them and, in this case, typically the Irish. If the person did not pay up the amount due in the note, the extortionists would beat them, kill them, burn their businesses to the ground, or hurt their families. But the Black Hand extortionists would still target other Italians, and when they decided to come after mob boss Big Jim Colosimo, that's when things got really ugly.

Colosimo was from Cosenza, Italy, having migrated to Chicago in 1895. He almost immediately began working alongside crooked Irish politicians, specifically a group called the Grey Wolves, who helped him open a brothel and kidnap young immigrant women, forcing them into a life of prostitution. By 1910, Colosimo had received more than his share of death threats from Black Hand extortionists who didn't like his involvement with the Irish, but he wasn't about to let these intimidation tactics impact his business.

New York mobster Johnny "the Fox" Torrio was a good friend of Colosimo and was happy to help "solve the problem" in Chicago when Big Jim called upon him for assistance. A battle broke out between the extortionists and Colosimo's gang, and within his first two months in Chicago, Torrio gunned down ten Black Hand members. Whether these murders happened by his own hand or through an accomplice, Torrio was instantly feared in the Chicago underworld.

All of this built up to a vicious war between the extortionists, the Italians, and the Irish, much of which unfolded at the menacing "Death Corner." The intersection at Oak Street and Milton Street (now Cleveland Street) received its name for the murders that occurred there. Gang members could easily get away with shooting another person in broad daylight, resulting in an average of thirty deaths every year. Onlookers weren't even paid to shut their mouths when police came looking for answers; they kept silent because they were terrified that their fate would be sealed if they ratted anyone out to the cops.

The Black Hand extortionists had a faceless gunman to do much of their dirty work, in order to keep themselves protected in case of arrests. The "Shotgun Man" was an unnamed assassin, notorious for carrying out the extortionists' sinister intentions. He was credited with the deaths of fifteen Italian immigrants at Death Corner between 1910 and 1911, and his name is now lost to history forever.

This tactic proved handy when Chicago police came through the neighborhood and rounded up anyone they thought had a connection to the gangs that roamed there.

Since the extortionists couldn't be connected to the meticulously crafted ransom notes they left, nor the faceless "Shotgun Man," many of them were set free, never to be charged with the murders they may have orchestrated. By the end of 1912, though, Colosimo's gang limited the power that the extortionists once had over wealthy Chicagoans, and members of the Black Hand slithered back into the unknown, rarely to be seen again in such masses.

But mob wars raged on. Between the Chicago Outfit, Torrio and Colosimo's new Italian formation, and the Irish Mob's North Side Gang, the Near North Side was crawling with gang members. Younger, fresher individuals would often work hard to gain favor with older, ill-famed gangs, desperately hoping there would be a place for them in the ranks once they proved themselves. For two decades, from 1910 through 1930, Chicago let these gangs run the streets, allowing terror and perversion to dictate politics, territory, and even personal relationships. The Near North Side struck fear into the average do-gooder, so much that they would never even think of trespassing through that side of town. That made the neighborhood a very inexpensive, albeit dangerous, place to live, and the cycle of poverty and systemic racism slipped into the recesses of the city.

African American families nearly all stemmed from low-income households at this point in history, suffering from the ignorant and usually cruel attitudes of white citizens. Many people refused to hire anyone black, worried that it would somehow taint their business or drive away paying customers. War was about the only industry that would hire

African American men, and it paid very little for exceptionally dangerous tasks.

When African American communities began to migrate to the Near North Side in the early 1930s, the Italian and Irish Mobs did not approve. Black people were targeted by the mobs, often beaten senseless or killed by gang members who were determined to stake their claim in the neighborhood. Still, the violence continued without interruption from Chicago politicians. That is, until 1942, when the Chicago Housing Authority (CHA) came up with a solution to the housing and crime crises.

The Frances Cabrini Homes were constructed: a small community of lower-income rowhouses that marked a square territory with Clybourn Avenue on the north, Chicago Avenue on the south, Orleans Street on the east, and Halsted Street on the west. Built just minutes from Chicago's higher-class neighborhoods—River North, Old Town, and Gold Coast—the project failed to benefit minority populations and the Near North Side remained one of the most infamous areas for gang violence.

During the construction of Cabrini's fifty-five two- and three-story buildings, many old slum houses and apartment buildings were torn down to make way for newer, affordable housing for the city's poor. While this sounds good in theory, the CHA had high standards for who it would let into its 586 units at Cabrini Homes. The residences were much more attractive than slum living, so there was instantly a high demand to get a spot on the waiting list. Much of the community being wiped out by this project could not even hope to apply, having criminal backgrounds, unstable income, or terrible credit to their name. As a result, Cabrini's initial residential population was only about 25 percent black when it was completed in 1945.

But then the war ended, bringing thousands of African American men home without foreseeable jobs. The war industry had exhausted its resources, kept its white employees, and sent black men off to a life of poverty. Many of them moved into Cabrini Homes, where residency was cheap. But these destitute men still needed a sustainable source of income in order to survive, even if it meant turning to criminal activity.

Drug sales began to run rampant in Cabrini Homes and addicts swarmed into the neighborhood just to get their hands on highly illegal substances from the dealers who lived there. This generated a bad name for the Near North Side once again, even though the perpetrators just needed a way to get by. The Italian Mafia still blamed the corruption of the neighborhood on black youth, constantly spreading violence in this new drug center and provoking African American gangs to move in and fight back. The controlling black gangs at the time included the Mickey Cobras, Gangster Disciples, Vice Lords, Imperial Chaplains, Fourteenth Street Clovers, and Black Disciples. Italian street gangs also formed and kept a constant race war in flux at Cabrini Homes throughout the 1940s, but that all changed at the start of the '50s.

Most white families experienced an upward swing in income and living standards throughout the second half of the twentieth century—especially in the wake of workforce inequality between white and black people—so many of them no longer needed public housing. This allowed more poverty-stricken black people to move into Cabrini Homes while the Italians moved out.

Crime was increasing near Cabrini Homes in the 1950s, but city officials counted the project as a success nonetheless. We can only speculate that it was considered successful because white people were no longer being killed in the crossfire of gang violence. It didn't matter how many black people were murdered; white people were safe and, therefore, the housing project was working. This racist sentiment still exists in Chicago today, where crime runs rampant and nothing is done about it.

Because Cabrini Homes made sense in the eyes of city officials, they held a discussion in 1950 with the CHA to decide where they would build more public housing, specifically to shelter the rising number of African American people migrating north. The CHA brought several vacant areas to the table, but it was generally felt that low-income public housing couldn't be built bordering white neighborhoods. Instead, the Chicago city council proposed that they demolish existing black-dominated slums, replacing them with high-rises that could house large quantities of people, and their vote won out. The repercussions of this decision have dramatically affected Chicago public housing into the twenty-first century.

Crime continued to crawl the streets around Cabrini Homes and its newest additions, the Cabrini Extension and the William Green Homes, throughout the 1950s and '60s. By 1962, the expanded projects were called Cabrini-Green, as they're more commonly known today. But the faux glory of Chicago public housing came to a sudden end on July 17, 1970, when two Chicago police officers were shot and killed by a sniper in one of the Cabrini-Green Homes. City officials could no longer pretend that Cabrini-Green was a good idea. Its streets were officially dangerous because they had stolen the lives of two white men.

For the next two decades, controversy erupted around the Cabrini-Green housing project. The area was regarded as a no-go zone and avoided at all costs. The dire state of Cabrini-Green was in the full light of public awareness, and Chicagoans wanted to put an end to the crime that was spilling from the front steps of public housing. Mayor Jane Byrne even famously moved into a housing unit in 1981 to bring about change at the front lines. However, her three weeks of effort to boost morale with a sports complex and to implement a variety of city services did very little for the community and ended entirely when she fell short of reelection in 1983.

All of the CHA's public housing complexes were torn down between 2000 and 2010 following the agency's 1999 Plan for Transformation, which mandated the replacement of low-income developments with mixed-income homes. But Chicago still remembers the blatant segregation that Cabrini-Green enforced upon its streets; much of it still impacts the city today.

BIBLIOGRAPHY

Johnson, Raymond, and Kimberly MacAulay. *Chicago History: The Stranger Side: Fact, Fiction, Folklore and "Fantoms" of the Windy City*. Atglen, PA: Schiffer Publishing, 2013.

Lombardo, Robert M. *Organized Crime in Chicago: Beyond the Mafia*. Urbana: University of Illinois Press, 2013.

Miller, Donald L. *City of the Century: The Epic of Chicago and the Making of America*. New York: RosettaBooks, 2014.

Taylor, Troy, Adam Selzer, and Ken Melvoin-Berg. *Weird Chicago: Forgotten History, Strange Legends & Mysterious Hauntings of the Windy City*. Chicago: Whitechapel Press, 2009.

Chapter 1: H. H. Holmes: Born with the Devil Inside

Crighton, J. D. *Detective in the White City: The Real Story of Frank Geyer*. Murrieta, CA: RW Publishing House, 2017.

Di Cola, Joseph M., and David Stone. *Chicago's 1893 World's Fair*. Charleston, SC: Arcadia, 2012.

Frey, Holly, and Tracy Wilson. "H. H. Holmes and the Mysteries of Murder Castle" (2 parts). *Stuff You Missed in History Class* (podcast), January 25, 2012.

History.com editors. "Murder Castle." A&E Television Networks, July 13, 2017. https://www.history.com/topics/crime/murder -castle.

Jenkins, John Philip. "H. H. Holmes: American Serial Killer." *Encyclopedia Britannica*. New York: Black Dog & Leventhal Publishers, 2008.

Killelea, Eric. "Serial Killer H. H. Holmes' Body Exhumed: What We Know." *Rolling Stone*, May 4, 2007.

Larson, Erik. *The Devil in the White City: Murder, Magic, and Madness at the Fair That Changed America*. Brantford, Ontario: W. Ross MacDonald School Research Services Library, 2016.

Selzer, Adam. *H. H. Holmes: The True History of the White City Devil*. New York: Skyhorse Publishing, 2019.

Chapter 2: The Everleigh Club: The Lavish Brothel in Chicago's Red-Light District

Abbott, Karen. *Sin in the Second City: Madams, Ministers, Playboys, and the Battle for America's Soul*. New York: Random House, 2008.

Aron, Nina Renata. "Meet the Sisters Who Ran 'the Most Famous and Luxurious House of Prostitution in the Country.'" *Timeline*, April 16, 2017.

Blair, Cynthia M. *I've Got to Make My Livin': Black Women's Sex Work in Turn-of-the-Century Chicago*. Chicago: The University of Chicago Press, 2018.

Kiernan, Louise. "The Everleigh Club." *Chicago Tribune*, December 19, 2007. https://www.chicagotribune.com/nation-world/chi-chicagodays-everleighclub-story-story.

Richardson, Vanessa, and Sami Nye. "The Everleigh Club—Ada and Minna Simms" (2 parts). *Female Criminals* (podcast), June 19, 2019.

Taylor, Troy. *Murder and Mayhem in Chicago's Vice Districts*. Charleston, SC: History Press, 2009.

Chapter 3: Al Capone: Chicago's Most Glorified Criminal

Bair, Deirdre. *Al Capone: His Life, Legacy, and Legend*. New York: Random House, 2017.

Bergreen, Laurence. *Capone: The Man and the Era*. New York: Simon and Schuster, 1994.

Binder, John J. *The Chicago Outfit*. Charleston, SC: Arcadia, 2003.

Curran, Oisin. "How 'Scarface' Al Capone Became the Original Gangster." *How Stuff Works* (blog). How Stuff Works. https://history.howstuffworks.com/history-vs-myth/capone-tax-evasion.htm.

Frey, Holly, and Tracy Wilson. 2012. "Public Enemies: 5 Gangsters to Know." *Stuff You Missed in History Class* (podcast), January 9, 2012.

History.com editors. "Al Capone." A&E Television Networks, October 14, 2009. https://www.history.com/topics/crime/al-capone.

Iorizzo, Luciano J. *Al Capone: A Biography*. London: Arachne Publishing, 2006.

Kobler, John. *Capone: The Life and World of Al Capone*. Cambridge, MA: Da Capo, 2003.

Chapter 4: John Dillinger:
Gunshots at Biograph Theater

Cromie, Robert Allen, and Joseph Pinkston. *Dillinger: A Short and Violent Life*. New York: McGraw-Hill, 1990.

Federal Bureau of Investigation, US Department of Justice. "John Dillinger." https://www.fbi.gov/history/famous-cases/john-dillinger.

Frey, Holly, and Tracy Wilson. "John Dillinger: Public Enemy Number One." *Stuff You Missed in History Class* (podcast), December 5, 2011.

Girardin, G. Russell, and William J. Helmer. *Dillinger: The Untold Story*. Bloomington: Indiana University Press, 2009.

Gorn, Elliott J. *Dillinger's Wild Ride: The Year That Made America's Public Enemy Number One*. Oxford: Oxford University Press, 2011.

"John Dillinger: American Gangster." *Encyclopedia Britannica*. New York: Black Dog and Leventhal, 2008.

King, Jeffery S. *The Rise and Fall of the Dillinger Gang*. Nashville: Cumberland House, 2005.

Matera, Dary. *John Dillinger: The Life and Death of America's First Celebrity Criminal*. New York: Barnes & Noble, 2007.

Toland, John. *The Dillinger Days*. New York: Da Capo Press, 1995.

Chapter 5: William Heirens: Questionable Conviction of the Lipstick Killer

Innes, Brian. *Serial Killers: Shocking, Gripping True Crime Stories of the Most Evil Murders*. London: Quercus Publishing, 2017.

Kennedy, Dolores. *William Heirens: His Day in Court*. Chicago: Bonus Books, 1991.

Kilgariff, Karen, and Georgia Hardstark. "Fingers Everywhere" (episode 119). *My Favorite Murder* (podcast), May 3, 2018.

Chapter 6: John Wayne Gacy: The Clown Killer's Reign of Terror

Amirante, Sam L. *John Wayne Gacy: Defending a Monster*. New York: Skyhorse Publishing, 2015.

History.com editors. "John Wayne Gacy Confesses to Dozens of Murders." A&E Television Networks, November 13, 2009. https://www.history.com/this-day-in-history/john-wayne-gacy-confesses.

Kilgariff, Karen, and Georgia Hardstark. "Live from the Chicago Podcast Festival" (episode 44). *My Favorite Murder* (podcast), November 23, 2016.

Linedecker, Clifford L. *The Man Who Killed Boys*. New York: St. Martins, 2003.

Silman, Jon. "How Did John Wayne Gacy Fit into the Origin of the 'Evil Clown'?" Oxygen.com, October 29, 2018.

Sullivan, Terry, and Peter T. Maiken. *Killer Clown: The John Wayne Gacy Murders*. New York: Windsor Publishing, 2013.

Ullman, Tracy. "Chicago's Secrets about John Wayne Gacy." *HuffPost*, May 6, 2013. https://www.huffpost.com/entry/ john-wayne-gacy-investigation_b_2775342.

Chapter 7: Homey D. Clown: How an Urban Legend Sparked Real Fear

Carreon, Joan. "School Officials: 'Homey' Spottings May Be." *Times of Northwest Indiana*, October 17, 1991. https://www .nwitimes.com/uncategorized/school-officials-homey-spottings -may-be/article_5ae6936e-d987-560f-b5b9-4e244f0717ce .html.

Johnson, Allan. "Police Taking Clown Sightings Seriously." *Chicago Tribune*, October 11, 1991. https://www.chicagotribune.com/ news/ct-xpm-1991-10-11-9104010895-story.html.

Recktenwald, William. "922 Homicides Made 1991 Year to Forget." *Chicago Tribune*, January 1, 1992. https://www.chicagotribune .com/news/ct-xpm-1992-01-01-9201010135-story.html.

Romano, Aja. "The Great Clown Panic of 2016 Is a Hoax. But the Terrifying Side of Clowns Is Real." *Vox*, October 12, 2016. https://www.vox.com/culture/2016/10/12/13122196/ clown-panic-hoax-history.

Thompson, Isaiah. "Urban Legends: Who Saw Homey the Clown?" *Chicago Reader*, October 26, 2006. https://www.chicagoreader .com/chicago/urban-legends-who-saw-homey-the-clown/ Content?oid=923500.

Chapter 8: The Treaty of Chicago: Uprooting the Potawatomi Tribe

Drake, Samuel G. *The Book of the Indians, or, Biography and History of the Indians of North America: From Its First Discovery to the Year 1841*. Boston: B. B. Mussey, 1845.

Hautzinger, Daniel. "'We're Still Here': Chicago's Native Amer- ican Community." WTTW Chicago. WFMT, November

9, 2018. https://interactive.wttw.com/playlist/2018/11/08/
native-americans-chicago.

History.com editors. "Native American History Timeline." A&E
Television Networks, November 27, 2018. https://www.history
.com/topics/native-american-history/native-american-timeline.

Office of the Historian, US Department of State. "Indian Treaties
and the Removal Act of 1830." Accessed September 28, 2019.
https://history.state.gov/milestones/1830-1860/indian-treaties.

Quaife, Milo Milton. *Chicago and the Old Northwest, 1673–1835,
a Study of the Evolution of the Northwestern Frontier; Together
with a History of Fort Dearborn*. Chicago: University of Chicago Press, 1913.

Chapter 9: Lager Beer Riot:
Immigrant Power against Ethnic Bias

Einhorn, Robin. "Lager Beer Riot." *Encyclopedia of Chicago*. Chicago: Chicago Historical Society, 2005.

Grossman, Ron. "Chicago's Lager Beer Riot Proved Immigrants'
Power." *Chicago Tribune*, September 25, 2015. https://www
.chicagotribune.com/history/ct-know-nothing-party-lager
-beer-riot-per-flashback-jm-20150925-story.html.

Hogan, John F., and Judy E. Brady. *The Great Chicago Beer Riot:
How Lager Struck a Blow for Liberty*. Charleston, SC: History
Press, 2015.

Lindberg, Richard. *To Serve and Collect: Chicago Politics and Police
Corruption from the Lager Beer Riot to the Summerdale Scandal:
1855–1960*. Carbondale: Southern Illinois University Press,
2008.

Chapter 10: The Great Chicago Fire:
The Lawless Aftermath

Boda, John, and Raymond Johnson. *The Great Chicago Fire*.
Charleston, SC: Arcadia, 2017.

History.com editors. "Chicago Fire of 1871." A&E Television Networks, March 4, 2010. https://www.history.com/topics/19th-century/great-chicago-fire.

Schons, Mary. "The Chicago Fire of 1871 and the 'Great Rebuilding.'" *National Geographic*, January 25, 2011. https://www.nationalgeographic.org/news/chicago-fire-1871-and-great-rebuilding/.

Wiltz, Teresa. "The Chicago Fire." *Chicago Tribune*, December 18, 2007. https://www.chicagotribune.com/nation-world/chi-chicagodays-fire-story-story.html.

Chapter 11: *The* Eastland *Disaster:*
Lake Michigan's Deadliest Shipwreck

Bonansinga, Jay R. *The Sinking of the Eastland: America's Forgotten Tragedy*. New York: Citadel Press, 2005.

Hilton, George W. *Eastland: Legacy of the* Titanic. Stanford, CA: Stanford University Press, 2005.

Stanahan, Susan Q. "The *Eastland* Disaster Killed More Passengers Than the *Titanic* and the *Lusitania*. Why Has It Been Forgotten?" *Smithsonian*, October 27, 2014.

Wachholz, Ted. *The Eastland Disaster*. Charleston, SC: Arcadia, 2005.

Chapter 12: *The Grimes Sisters:*
The Cold Case That Shocked the Nation

Bovsun, Mara. "Sixty Years Later, the Case of the Elvis Presley–Loving Grimes Sisters' Murders Remains Cold." *New York Daily News*, April 8, 2018. https://www.nydailynews.com/news/crime/elvis-presley-loving-grimes-sisters-found-dead-60-years-article-1.2922567.

*Chicago Tribune*s. "Autopsy Widens Mystery." January 24, 1957.

———. "Hunt for 2 Lost Girls Intensified by Police." January 4, 1957.

———. "'I Knew It!' Sobs Mother." January 23, 1957.

———. "Widen Search for 2 Young Sisters Missing Four Days." January 1, 1957.

———. "Young Sisters Reported Seen in Two Places." December 31, 1956.

Lowry, Shirley. "Lost Girls' Mother Keeps Brave." *Chicago Tribune*, January 11, 1957.

Newton, Michael. *The Encyclopedia of Unsolved Crimes*. New York: Checkmark Books, 2010.

Taylor, Troy. *True Crime, Illinois: The State's Most Notorious Criminal Cases*. Mechanicsburg, PA: Stackpole Books, 2009.

Zorn, Eric. "2 Friends Dig into a 41-Year-Old Deadly Mystery." *Chicago Tribune,* December 23, 1997. https://www.chicago tribune.com/news/ct-xpm-1997-12-23-9712230046-story .html.

Chapter 13: Teresita Basa: The Voice from the Grave

HowStuffWorks editors. "The Strange Case of Teresita Basa." *Stuff They Don't Want You to Know* (podcast), YouTube video, August 6, 2016. https://youtu.be/hfYBteQDwb8.

O'Brien, John, and Edward Baumann. *Teresita, the Voice from the Grave: The Incredible but True Story of How an Occult Vision Solved the Murder of Teresita Basa*. Chicago: Bonus Books, 1992.

Rice, Linze. "Did Teresita Basa Solve Her Own Murder? True Life Ghost Story Still Haunts." DNAinfo Chicago, September 13, 2016. https://www.dnainfo.com/chicago/20160913/edgewater/ did-teresita-basa-solve-her-own-murder-true-life-ghost-story -still-haunts.

Chapter 14: Flight 191: The Deadliest Plane Crash in Chicago History

Benzkofer, Stephan. "Worst Plane Crash in US History." *Chicago Tribune*, May 25, 2014. https://www.chicagotribune.com/

news/ct-1979-ohare-crash-flashback-0525-20140525-story
.html.

Korovin, Igor. *The Worst Single Plane Crash in American History: The Crash of American Airlines Flight 191*. Self-published, Lulu .com, 2011.

Lowe, Mike. "Flight 191 Crash, 40 Years Later: Victims' Loved Ones Mark Anniversary with Somber Memorial." WGN Chicago, May 21, 2019. https://wgntv.com/2019/05/21/loved -ones-of-flight-191-victims-to-mark-crash-anniversary-with -somber-memorial/.

Mann, Julie. "Rewind-Fast Forward: Flight 191, Boeing 737 Max and Aviation Safety." WBBM News Radio, May 23, 2019. https://wbbm780.radio.com/rewind-fast-forward-flight -191.

McCoppin, Robert. "Hundreds Gather at Memorial Service to Honor the 273 People Killed 40 Years Ago When Flight 191 Crashed at O'Hare." *Chicago Tribune*, May 25, 2019. https://www.chicagotribune.com/news/breaking/ct-met-flight -191-memorial-20190525-story.html.

Negroni, Christine. *Crash Detectives: Investigating the World's Most Mysterious Air Disasters*. London: Atlantic Books, 2018.

Smith, Bryan. "The Ghosts of Flight 191." *Chicago*, May 7, 2019.

Chapter 15: Lincoln Park:
The Skeletal History That Lies Beneath

Bannos, Pamela. "Hidden Truths: The Chicago City Cemetery and Lincoln Park." Northwestern University. Accessed September 29, 2019. http://hiddentruths.northwestern.edu/home .html.

Loerzel, Robert. 2008. "A Conservatory, a Zoo, and 12,000 Corpses." *Chicago Reader*, May 15, 2008. https://www.chicago-reader.com/chicago/a-conservatory-a-zoo-and-12000-corpses/ Content?oid=1109775.

Chapter 16: The Iroquois Theatre Fire: The Alley of Death and Mutilation

Atlas Obscura. "Chicago's 'Alley of Death.'" January 25, 2018. https://www.atlasobscura.com/places/couch-place-the-alley-of-death.

Everett, Marshall. *Lest We Forget: Chicago's Awful Theater Horror.* Charleston, SC: Nabu Press, 2012.

Hatch, Anthony P. *Tinder Box: The Iroquois Theatre Disaster, 1903.* Chicago: Academy Chicago Publishers, 2010.

Keegan, Anne. "Tales of the Crypt." *Chicago Tribune,* January 3, 1993. https://www.chicagotribune.com/news/ct-xpm-1993-01-03-9303150301-story.html.

Chapter 17: The Green Mill: Mob Mentality at Chicago's Top Jazz Club

Atlas Obscura. "Green Mill Jazz Club: Chicago's Premier Prohibition-Era Jazz Club Is Still Running." February 23, 2017. https://www.atlasobscura.com/places/green-mill.

Chicago Tribune. "Cabaret Man's Fears Told as Stabbing Clew." November 9, 1927.

Kirouac, Matt. "A Look Inside Chicago's Historic Green Mill Lounge." Culture Trip, August 27, 2018. https://theculturetrip.com/north-america/usa/illinois/articles/a-look-inside-the-historic-green-mill-lounge/.

Sisson, Patrick. "An Oral History of the Green Mill." *Chicago Reader,* March 20, 2014. https://www.chicagoreader.com/chicago/uptown-greenmilljazz-bar-history-owner-bartender-musicians/Content?oid=12784766.

Taylor, Troy. *Murder and Mayhem on Chicago's North Side.* Charleston, SC: History Press, 2009.

Chapter 18: Lottie's Pub: The Secret Rathskeller Owned by Chicago's Intersex Heroine

Ben-Amots, Zach. "Chicago Corner Bar Lottie's Pub Turns 85, Relic of Historic Bucktown." ABC7 Chicago, May 22, 2019. https://abc7chicago.com/food/lotties-pub-in-bucktown-turns -85/5311560/.

LaMorte, Chris. "Digging Up the Past." *Chicago Tribune*, October 29, 2004. https://www.chicagotribune.com/news/ct-xpm -2004-10-29-0410300074-story.html.

Chapter 19: Cabrini Homes: Systemic Racism and Gang Violence in Chicago's First Slum

Asbury, Herbert. *The Gangs of Chicago: An Informal History of the Chicago Underworld*. London: Arrow, 2003.

Austen, Ben. "'They Don't Live Very Fancy Here at Cabrini.'" *Chicago*, February 2018. https://www.chicagomag.com/ Chicago-Magazine/February-2018/Cabrini-Green/.

"Cabrini-Green." *Encyclopedia Britannica*. New York: Black Dog and Leventhal, 2008.

Marriott, Laura. "Welcoming the Mayor to Hell: The Story of Jane Byrne and Cabrini Green." HeadStuff, January 15, 2017. https://www.headstuff.org/culture/history/cabrini-green -mayor-jane-byrne/.

Modica, Aaron. "Cabrini Green Housing Project, Chicago, Illinois (1942–2009)." BlackPast, July 26, 2019. https://www.black past.org/african-american-history/cabrini-green-housing -project-chicago-1942-2009/.

Voegeli, William. "Public Housing's Most Notorious Failure." *City Journal*, August 19, 2018. https://www.city-journal.org/html/ cabrini-green-homes-16037.html.

About the Author

Kali Joy Cramer graduated with a B.A. in English and Communications in 2016. Out of college, she took a job as a content writer for two years before moving on to become editor-in-chief for *UrbanMatter*, a digital Chicago-based nightlife and entertainment guide. Kali's work has also been published through *Chicago Scene* magazine.

She currently lives in Pilsen, a neighborhood that she feels fosters a strong connection to Chicago. On the weekends, Kali enjoys reading in the sunroom, exploring her neighborhood, observing art and theater, and finding little moments of peace in the midst of this busy life.